What people are saying...

Pastor Aaron Lewis is truly a man of God. He is a man under the mandate of the Lord, anointed to sharpen the views we have of the kingdom of God and our place in that kingdom. He has taken his pastoral anointing, coupled with the wisdom that God has unleashed through him, to create a work that can be appreciated and applied by people from many various walks of life. In a broader sense, this book contains elements that would be helpful to all mankind.

I have been in services where Aaron has ministered and have always come away feeling inspired to live a better life because of what God imparted to me through him. Aaron is now making this same impartation available in book form. I believe that *Healing for the 21st Century* is destined to be an international best-seller because of the valuable message it communicates.

—Jack Coe, Jr.
International Healing Evangelist &
President, Christian Fellowship
Dallas, Texas

Aaron Lewis' book, *Healing for the 21st Century,* does a wonderful job of speaking to the twenty-first century church about God's will to heal His body.

After I finished reading the book, I knew that I had hold of a message that impacted me greatly. Most of it was underlined, and there were notes all over the margins. This is just that kind of book. *Healing for the 21st Century* deals with issues that for many decades we have swept underneath the carpet. If we are going to see healing as normal an experience as salvation is within the body, we must come into the revelation of everything that is provided in the Atonement. Aaron Lewis shows us that God is not only able to heal us, but He is equally as willing.

—*Rev. Cal Pierce*
Director, Healing Rooms Ministries
Spokane, Washington

AARON D. LEWIS

Whitaker House

visit our website at:
www.21stcenturyhealer.com

Unless otherwise noted, all Scripture quotations are taken from
the New King James Version (NKJV) © 1979, 1980, 1982 by
Thomas Nelson, Inc. Used by permission. All rights reserved.

Scripture quotations marked (KJV) are taken from the King
James Version of the Holy Bible.

Editorial note: Because we do not wish to give the enemy any
additional attention, we have chosen not to capitalize any of his
alternative names in this work.

The information presented here is not intended as medical advice.
Always consult your physician before undertaking any change in
your physical regimen, whether fasting, diet, or exercise.

HEALING FOR THE 21ST CENTURY

You may contact the author at:
21st Century Resources
P.O. Box 8286
Manchester, CT 06040-0286

ISBN: 0-88368-653-8
Printed in the United States of America
Copyright © 2000 by Aaron D. Lewis

Whitaker House
30 Hunt Valley Circle
New Kensington, PA 15068

Library of Congress Cataloging-in-Publication Data

Lewis, Aaron D., 1969–
   Healing for the 21st century / by Aaron D. Lewis.
      p. cm.
   ISBN 0-88368-653-8 (pbk. : alk. paper)
   1.   Spiritual healing.   I. Title: Healing for the twenty-first
   century. II. Title.
BT732.5 .L45 2001
234'.131—dc21   00-012771

   1 2 3 4 5 6 7 8 9 10 11 12 / 09 08 07 06 05 04 03 02 01 00

contents

Acknowledgments 9

Introduction...11

1. God Wants You to Be Healed! 15

2. It's a Matter of Flesh and Blood 35

3. *Now* Faith..53

4. The Thief of Religion 71

5. Words Count 99

6. The Healing–Anointing Connection 117

7. Scriptural Methods of Healing 137

8. Atmosphere Is Everything............................163

9. Hindrances to Healing 179

10. Maintaining Your Healing 189

Afterthoughts: Your God-given Destiny 201

About the Author 205

Dedication

To all of the people of the world who have yet
to discover Christ's unlimited power to heal.

Acknowledgments

As I ponder the potential of this project and the many lives that will be positively affected by what is written here, I am reminded of the words of Frederick Douglass, the nineteenth-century African-American spokesperson, abolitionist, reformer, author, and orator: "We are one, our cause is one, and we must help each other, if we are to succeed." Douglass provokes us to realize just how much our successes are connected by interwoven threads of our past and our present through the contributions of the many people who have helped to refine us.

With that in mind, there are hundreds of people who have sown their time, talents, and treasures into my life, for which I am grateful. While space prevents me from acknowledging every contributor over the course of my life, there are those who have made such significant deposits that they are noteworthy to mention here:

My loving wife, Tiwanna, who creates an atmosphere of glory in my life, which helps me to produce literary, audio, and visual resources that influence the world. Your faithfulness to God, to me, to our children, and to the universal church continually humbles me.

My parents, Bishop Austin and Rev. Martha Lewis, who gave me the gift of life, which makes it possible for me to share life with others.

The anointed ministers Dr. Creflo A. Dollar, Jr., Dr. Myles Munroe, Benny Hinn, Bishop Earl

Paulk, Dr. Frederick K. C. Price, Kenneth Cope-
land, Oral Roberts, and Bishop T. D. Jakes, Sr.,
whose spiritual gifts and deposits have made me
more conscious of the potential of a seed and the
power of a purpose-driven life.

Dr. LeRoy Bailey, Jr., and the First Cathedral family for their consistent support and prayers. It was at the First Cathedral that I facilitated
the very first School of Healing, out of which the
concept for *Healing for the 21st Century* was en-
visaged.

The covenant members and the leadership
team of The Family of God, on whom I had the
privilege of testing and sharing the life-changing
thoughts in these pages.

The fine family at Whitaker House Publish-
ers, especially Jim Rill, Shicara Shaw, and
Sharon Hemingway, whose efforts helped to bring
this work to fruition.

> *But as his part is who goes down to the
> battle, so shall his part be who stays by
> the supplies; they shall share alike.*
> (1 Samuel 30:24)

The godly principle of our being one body
with one cause was eloquently stated by Frederick Douglass. From David's above declaration we
derive the additional principle that, as the army of
the Lord, we share in the work of the battle, no
matter how menial the task or how unnoticed our
contributions may be, and therefore we should all
share in the spoils of victory. Thus, I share the
eternal fruits of this endeavor with all of you, my
friends and *"fellow laborer[s] in the gospel of
Christ"* (1 Thessalonians 3:2).

Introduction

Jesus Christ is the same yesterday,
today, and forever.
—Hebrews 13:8

In 1969, when I was born, times were considerably different than they are now. The United States was just beginning to adjust to the drastic racial equality changes that the civil rights movement engendered. Richard Nixon was inaugurated as president of the United States and announced the beginning of troop withdrawal from Vietnam. The average home in 1969 cost approximately $40,000. Today the average home exceeds $160,000 in many areas of the United States. A fully equipped automobile retailed for about $2000. We would be very fortunate today to find a quality used car for that amount. Back then, gasoline averaged $.32 a gallon, a far cry from the prices we pay at the pumps now.

Without much reflection, we can easily recognize that times have changed. Some changes have been for our overall benefit. Other changes have benefited the so-called dominant group at the expense of the underprivileged.

Notwithstanding all of these transitions, one thing remains constant and never changing—the Word of God. In accordance with Scripture, I submit that the Word of God and the Lord Jesus Christ are one and the same.

In the beginning was the Word, and the Word was with God, and the Word was God. (John 1:1)

By accepting this truth, we must also realize that the Word of God is incapable of changing. As Hebrews 13:8 declares, *"Jesus Christ is the same yesterday, today, and forever."* In order for God's Word to change, God Himself must change. Yet if God were to change His nature, His name, or His Word, all humanity and creation would cease to exist as they do now. Luke 16:17 states, *"And it is easier for heaven and earth to pass away than for one tittle of the law* [God's Word] *to fail."* Another way to look at this is that the heavens and the entire earthly realm will die if the smallest word from God does not come to pass. God wagered the entire universe on the integrity of His Word. God has constrained Himself by His Word, and He will always remain faithful to do exactly what He says He will do.

It is obvious that God has various expressions and multifaceted methods of revealing Himself to humanity. We must understand that God's quality of being the same does not mean that He is unable to bring about revival, restoration, or a fresh new move; rather, it means that He remains constant in His character. God's character never changes and will always remain the same.

When we think of God doing a new thing, we must not lower His divinity to our mortal standards by believing that anything He has done previously is obsolete. God never ages, and in Him there is no regression. What we consider to be new from God is merely an ever existing expression of God that we have not perceived yet, because of our spiritual blindness. What we consider new revelations have always been in God. They become new to us at the moment we perceive them with our spiritual understanding.

One aspect of God's unchanging character is His will for everyone to be healed of sickness. Just as it is His will for all to be saved, He has always desired to bring healing to everyone. Yet millions—perhaps even billions—remain ignorant concerning God's will for His creation. In so many cases, people do not die of debilitating illnesses, premature death, or congenital diseases by fluke or coincidence. These sicknesses are brought to full term because of ignorance—in other words, a lack of knowledge.

> *My people are destroyed for lack of knowledge. Because you have rejected knowledge, I also will reject you from being priest for Me; because you have forgotten the law of your God, I also will forget your children.*　　(Hosea 4:6)

Interestingly enough, Scripture reveals that the destruction of people can be directly correlated to a lack of knowledge. Lack of knowledge destroys not only people, but also spirituality, marriages, relationships, families, financial stability, and health. According to Scripture, it seems that the destructive nature of our ignorance may be passed down to our children. How unfortunate it is to pass a curse to an unborn child awaiting entry into the world simply because we failed to acquire knowledge.

Digest this truth: God's Word states that the underlying cause of our ruination and destruction is lack of knowledge. If your loved ones died before God's appointed time for them to die, they did not die prematurely because of a lack of medical expertise. They didn't die because of a shortage of pharmaceuticals. They did not die because of a lack of a cure for whatever sickness that ailed them. Unfortunately, they departed from this life because they lacked knowledge on how they could sustain life and fulfill their God-given destiny.

You, my readers, will never lack this knowledge that many have wanted but never pursued. In your hands you hold knowledge and potential power. This work, *Healing for the 21st Century,* will serve as a companion to the Holy Bible as it relates to healing for your body. By heeding the instructions in this book, as they are dependent on God's Word, by watering this information with faith, and by believing the words that God spoke, I am certain that you will receive and maintain the healing that God so desires you to have. Read with faith and with an open mind; open your spirit, and receive your healing forever. Let the healing begin!

Read with faith and with an open mind; open your spirit, and receive your healing forever!

> *Wisdom is the principal thing; therefore get wisdom. And in all your getting, get understanding.* (Proverbs 4:7)

> *Beloved, I pray that you may prosper in all things and be in health, just as your soul prospers.* (3 John 2)

chapter one

God Wants You to Be Healed!

America is dying! Even more tragic is that America seems to be in denial concerning her condition. Although billions of dollars are being spent annually on health research, medication, and treatment, millions of Americans continue to die prematurely.

Leading Causes of Death

The United States of America is one of the world's leaders in manufacturing supplemental vitamins, minerals, and other health-related products. However, we lead many countries in the number of heart attacks, strokes, blood diseases, and cancer-related illnesses that occur each year. The *National Vital Statistics Reports* periodically issues an abridged listing of the causes of death in the United States.

Ten Leading Causes of Death in the U.S.
(1997, all ages)*

Heart disease: **726,974**
Cancer: **539,577**
Stroke: **159,791**

---

* *National Vital Statistics Reports,* Vol. 47, No. 19.

Chronic obstructive pulmonary disease: **109,029**
Accidents: **95,644**
Pneumonia/influenza: **84,449**
Diabetes: **62,636**
Suicide: **30,535**
Nephritis, nephrotic syndrome, nephrosis: **25,331**
Chronic liver disease and cirrhosis: **25,175**

Unquestionably, these figures are perturbing. They represent the deteriorating condition of our families, friends, loved ones, and ourselves. They also represent a need that is far too great for medical experts to deal with properly.

While doctors are susceptible to human error, our Creator cannot fail. We must realize that it is God's will, His desire, and His good pleasure for us to walk in divine health. God wants us to be healed!

A Deeper Look at 3 John 2

In his third epistle, the apostle John wrote to a church leader in one of the churches in Asia, a man by the name of Gaius. We do not have much information concerning the beloved Gaius. Nor do we know exactly which Gaius the apostle John was referring to, since Gaius was a common name in the Roman world. The name Gaius was as common at that time as the name Michael is today. Although we have limited knowledge about Gaius, we do have enough information to establish a strong precedent of God's willingness to heal.

Beloved, I pray that you may prosper in all things and be in health, just as your soul prospers. (3 John 2)

First, we recognize that John referred to Gaius as *"beloved."* The word *"beloved"* comes from the Greek word *agapetos.* Its root word is the word *agape,* which describes God's unfailing, unqualified, and unconditional love for human-kind. *Agapetos* is a greeting word that would be directed only toward someone who had a strong affinity with the writer. From this we can gather that Gaius was not just another church leader, but rather that he was someone John knew and loved deeply.

It is evident that John knew of Gaius's works in the church because he noted a few observations after he prayed for Gaius's health. First, he commended Gaius for living a Christian lifestyle so conscientiously that believers came to tell him about it.

> *For I rejoiced greatly when brethren came and testified of the truth that is in you, just as you walk in the truth. I have no greater joy than to hear that my children walk in truth.* (3 John 3–4)

Next, John praised Gaius, his son in the Lord, for walking in truth. What truth did Gaius walk in? He walked in the truth of God's Word. He lived a lifestyle of walking in and by the Word of God.

> *Beloved, you do faithfully whatever you do for the brethren and for strangers, who have borne witness of your love before the church. If you send them forward on their journey in a manner worthy of God, you will do well.* (3 John 5–6)

Here we read that John expressed his approval of Gaius for giving financial offerings to support itinerant preachers and the work of the ministry. The Scripture says that giving should be done in a manner worthy of God. As you would give to God, so should you give to His ministers who carry the Gospel of the kingdom.

We notice two powerful character traits of Gaius. First, he was a man who lived an honorable lifestyle. Second, he was generous and was thoroughly concerned about the work of the Lord.

The Scriptural Foundation

> *All Scripture is given by inspiration of God, and is profitable for doctrine, for reproof, for correction, for instruction in righteousness, that the man of God may be complete, thoroughly equipped for every good work.* (2 Timothy 3:16–17)

If these verses in Second Timothy are true—and they are—then we must receive John's good, prayerful instruction to Gaius, his son in the Lord, as God's good instruction for all of His children. All Scripture is given by God's inspiration. All Scripture has teaching content that will enable students to be fully equipped to accomplish the work God has for them to do.

> *Beloved, I wish above all things that thou mayest prosper and be in health, even as thy soul prospereth.* (3 John 2 KJV)

Through John's penned words to Gaius, God is telling us that He wants His children to be prosperous and healthy, first spiritually and then physically. When you are living a righteous life before God and your foremost priority is having a relationship with Christ, God wants you to be healed and to prosper *"above all things,"* as this verse reads in the King James Version. God has placed such great importance on these two things in your life because, without them, you would be limited in what you could realize for His kingdom.

Note what the Scripture does *not* say. It does not say, "I wish above all things that you may receive the baptism of the Holy Spirit." It does not say, "I wish above all things that you would prophesy and give words of knowledge." It does not say, "I wish above all things that you may live a lifestyle of prayer and fasting." All of these spiritual gifts and graces seem to have much more spiritual value than being healthy and prosperous. Why, then, would God place such a high priority on these two things?

Obviously, there are many reasons why God wants you to be healthy and whole. As our Father, God takes pleasure in giving His children the best, and this includes a healthy body and a prosperous life. There are other key reasons why God wants you to be healed. When Jesus gave the Great Commission, He made some interesting statements that are worth our attention.

> God takes pleasure in giving His children the best, and this includes a healthy body and a prosperous life.

> *And Jesus came and spoke to them, saying, "All authority has been given to Me in heaven and on earth. Go therefore and make disciples of all the nations, baptizing them in the name of the Father and of the Son and of the Holy Spirit, teaching them to observe all things that I have commanded you; and lo, I am with you always, even to the end of the age." Amen.* (Matthew 28:18–20)

In this passage, Jesus commands us to go out to the nations and make disciples, or followers of His teachings. Next, He wants us to baptize those disciples as an outward sign of an inward conversion. Finally, we are to teach them to do exactly what Christ has taught us to do. Jesus knew that if His disciples would do these things, then Christ's kingdom would be established throughout the world.

The Power to Get Wealth

Now let's look further into the biblical aspects of this subject.

> *And you shall remember the LORD your God, for it is He who gives you power to get wealth, that He may establish His covenant which He swore to your fathers, as it is this day.* (Deuteronomy 8:18)

God gives us *"power to get wealth,"* but not so we will hoard money or spend it wastefully. God gives the power to get wealth to those He can trust to reinvest the money back into the kingdom, so that His promises can be established.

> **God gives the power to get wealth to those He can trust to reinvest the money back into the kingdom.**

No wonder John prayed for Gaius to have health and financial well-being! Gaius was one of many disciples who would continue to support the cause of the kingdom with his financial gifts. If Gaius became ill, he would be drained of the physical and mental energy he needed to produce the wealth that was necessary to sustain the portion of the ministry that God had entrusted him to support. God desires for us to be in health, first, for the benefit of His kingdom, and then for our personal benefit.

Without the involvement of His children, God's purposes will never be accomplished, and His promises will never be fulfilled. This involvement demands that we be in optimum health, ready for the next assignment from the Captain of God's army, the Lord Jesus Christ. God wants you to be healed more than you want to be healed. God is waiting for you.

Forever Settled

Before we continue any further, one thing must be settled and certain in your mind: It is God's will for me to be healed; in fact, it is God's will for me to walk in divine health at all times.

If you are very sick and this statement stirs up doubt and disbelief in your soul, your battle for life may already be lost. You might as well choose your casket, select the floral arrangements, prepay your favorite mortician, and make a list of your favorite hymns. Without faith in God's will for your healing, you are easy prey for the spirit of death.

You may not yet know the methods and environment conducive for healing. However, your faith in the possibility of your healing is the very first step toward your attainment of that healing.

> But Jesus looked at them and said to them, "With men this is impossible, but with God all things are possible."
>
> (Matthew 19:26)

You cannot skip this step and go on to the more in-depth revelation concerning healing. You must start here.

Jesus said to him, "If you can believe, all things are possible to him who believes."
(Mark 9:23)

Over the past several years, I have had the privilege of praying for thousands of people who needed a healing touch from the Lord. From what I have observed, those who received their healing always seemed to have hope in God for their healing. Even if they were sinners, their minds moved far beyond their sinful state to the possibility that God just might heal them. The question with many of them was not if God *could* do it, but rather if God *would* do it for them.

Sadly, many born-again Christians question God's will and wonder if He will heal them. No doubt, God does not like this attitude. God has made it vividly clear what His Word says concerning healing, yet many of His children do not believe Him. They do not have faith in His Word. This lack of faith not only brings displeasure to God, but it also invalidates the good things that God has prepared for His children to receive.

But without faith it is impossible to please Him, for he who comes to God must believe that He is, and that He is a rewarder of those who diligently seek Him.
(Hebrews 11:6)

Have you ever heard this kind of lament: "God, why did You heal that sinner? After all, he doesn't even go to church. He's a chain smoker, an alcoholic, and a womanizer. I'm a Christian. I attend church regularly. God, that's just not fair"? I've heard these complaints from Christians more times than I can count. Each time I hear such complaints, they are always from a so-called believer who does not really believe—someone whose heart isn't right with God, but whose life appears to be full of religious activities and good works.

The one thing that many fail to recognize is that God does not respond to works alone. Healing comes to those who have true faith, and works that are independent of faith are meaningless works in the eyes of God. *"Even so faith, if it hath not works, is dead, being alone"* (James 2:17 KJV). Faith and works go together like wetness and water. You cannot have wetness without water in some form. You cannot have water in its normal state without wetness. Actions or works will always accompany the God-pleasing kind of faith. Works that will receive God's attention must be accompanied by faith.

Often, we Christians become so religious that we fail to remember that God requires total faith in His Word, regardless of how bleak the situation may appear. Sinners may see more healing than we do because they are willing to take the risk of faith, expecting the possibility of healing to manifest. Meanwhile, so-called religious believers process the Word of God, the commands of the Lord, and the prompting of His ministers to see if these things fit their personal dogmas and convictions. God doesn't give His best to those who do not yield themselves entirely to Him and have complete faith in Him.

> Sinners may see more healing than we do because they are willing to take the risk of faith, expecting the possibility of healing to manifest.

Please understand that I am not chastising anyone who examines what a minister preaches in light of the Word of God. I wholeheartedly agree with Paul's commendation of the Bereans for using the Scriptures as their foundation of truth from which they evaluated his teachings.

> [The Berean Jews] *were more fair-minded than those in Thessalonica, in that they received the word with all readiness, and searched the Scriptures daily to find out whether these things were so. Therefore many of them believed, and also not a few of the Greeks, prominent women as well as men.* (Acts 17:11–12)

However, I am saying that to twist and distort Scripture to fit a personal religious viewpoint defies and reverses the way we are to develop our belief systems, and is therefore wrong. Some "believers" try to mold the Word to fit their entrenched doctrines because they erroneously assert that they possess the only truth. Instead, we are supposed to start with the truth of God's Word and, through studying it, formulate and articulate our beliefs.

We have no right to assume that by our sanction of God's Word, we can actualize it. Our belief in what God has said does not make it true, because His Word is truth. However, our belief can make it true for us. We dare not dilute or limit God's Word with our puny opinions and restrictions, especially in regard to healing. Negative attitudes are likely to invalidate your healing. God is looking for someone to believe Him without reservations. Can He count on you?

> Our belief in what God has said does not make it true.... However, our belief can make it true for us.

Just a Little Faith, Please

Too often we try to compare our faith to the faith of those in Scripture and to modern-day achievers who have exemplified great faith. The process of comparing will always defeat your faith and leave you feeling as if you are totally worthless in God's eyes.

God does not need great faith in order to produce healing results in your life. He only needs faith. Regardless of the size of your faith, God can produce the miracle in you to move any mountain that has long been hindering your complete wholeness and restoration.

> So the Lord said, "If you have faith as a mustard seed, you can say to this mulberry tree, 'Be pulled up by the roots and be planted in the sea,' and it would obey you." (Luke 17:6)

This comparison of faith to a mustard seed deals with the potential of faith in its smallest form. Consider the nature of the mustard seed. Among seeds sown in a garden, the mustard seed is generally considered the smallest. But once the seed has taken root, it grows into a plant that reaches ten to fifteen feet in height. During the fall of the year, its branches become rigid, and the plant often becomes a place of shelter for birds of various species. It is amazing that this tiny seed can become a significant plant and a place of shelter.

We can learn this lesson from the mustard seed: What may seem small to you may be very big in God's eyes. All you need is just a little faith to invite God's presence and activate His healing in you. Your faith has the capacity to produce greatness far beyond what you can dream of.

> Your faith has the capacity to produce greatness far beyond what you can dream of.

Concerning our ideas about faith, we need to discover from Scripture that what is important is the presence of faith, not its strength.

> *And Peter answered Him and said, "Lord, if it is You, command me to come to You on the water." So He said, "Come." And when Peter had come down out of the boat, he walked on the water to go to Jesus. But when he saw that the wind was boisterous, he was afraid; and beginning to sink he cried out, saying, "Lord, save me!" And immediately Jesus stretched out His hand and caught him, and said to him, "O you of little faith, why did you doubt?" And when they got into the boat, the wind ceased. Then those who were in the boat came and worshiped Him, saying, "Truly You are the Son of God."* (Matthew 14:28–33)

Jesus referred to Peter as *"you of little faith."* Can you remember when you aspired to walk on water? I am not sure that anyone who believes in God so much that he would even attempt to walk on water would be considered a person with little faith. In fact, that act must have taken great faith.

The word *"little"* used here is derived from the Greek word *oligos,* which means "brief in extent or duration, short, small, or a while." Thus, when Jesus called Peter *"you of little faith,"* He meant that Peter's faith was great, but that it lasted for only a short while. *"Little faith"* is not a derogatory comment; rather, it refers to the duration of faith.

Often we hear a word from the Lord concerning our health and well-being. Unfortunately, our faith in this word is usually short-lived. It usually lasts until we surround ourselves with unbelieving "believers." It lasts for the duration of the service or of the audio or video cassette. It lasts until we come back down to what we call "reality." This kind of faith is what Jesus describes as *"little faith."* It's not the amount of faith you have, but the fact that you have it that counts. Will you stand in faith for your healing for the next year or two? At what point does your faith quit? Your faith will always produce results, whether it is large-quantity faith or small-quantity faith.

> *So Jesus answered and said to them, "Have faith in God. For assuredly, I say to you, whoever says to this mountain, 'Be removed and be cast into the sea,' and does not doubt in his heart, but believes that those things he says will be done, he will have whatever he says."*
> (Mark 11:22–23)

"Whoever" includes everybody! The only prerequisite to moving mountains is faith in God. You must be absolutely convinced that it is God's will to heal you. By the way, you do have the right amount of faith to get the job done.

The Battle Is in Your Mind

The greatest battle that you will face in attaining your healing will not be from external forces but rather from within. Your most significant encounter will not be the physical pain or the struggle for survival. Your primary battle will originate in the recesses of your mind. The Word of God has much to say concerning a person's thought life and the resulting manifestation of his thoughts. The following Scriptures may be hazardous to your religious tradition if it seeks to discount the validity, truth, and deliberateness of what God said and meant. Proceed with caution!

> *For as* [a man] *thinks in his heart, so is he.* (Proverbs 23:7)

> *Then Simeon blessed them, and said to Mary His mother, "Behold, this Child is destined for the fall and rising of many in Israel, and for a sign which will be spoken against (yes, a sword will pierce through your own soul also), that the thoughts of many hearts may be revealed."* (Luke 2:34–35)

> *Then the LORD saw that the wickedness of man was great in the earth, and that every intent of the thoughts of his heart was only evil continually.* (Genesis 6:5)

> *For the word of God is living and powerful, and sharper than any two-edged sword, piercing even to the division of soul and spirit, and of joints and marrow, and is a discerner of the thoughts and intents of the heart.* (Hebrews 4:12)

> *Search me, O God, and know my heart: try me, and know my thoughts.* (Psalm 139:23 KJV)

> *For "who has known the mind of the LORD that he may instruct Him?" But we have the mind of Christ.* (1 Corinthians 2:16)

As for you, my son Solomon, know the God of your father, and serve Him with a loyal heart ["perfect heart," KJV] and with a willing mind; for the LORD searches all hearts and understands all the intent of the thoughts. If you seek Him, He will be found by you; but if you forsake Him, He will cast you off forever. (1 Chronicles 28:9)

At this very moment you are who you think you are. You have what you think you deserve. You are the manifestation of the constant processing of your thoughts. Change what you think, and you will change your entire life. *"For as [a man] thinks in his heart, so is he"* (Proverbs 23:7). Do you really think you are sick? Or is that the message that your mind has been sending to your physical realm?

The reality is that you are what God says you are. God says you are healed. The only thing that can abrogate that statement is concentrating on the physical realm and the sense realm more than on God's Word. You will inevitably become what you concentrate on.

If you think and meditate on the negative diagnosis that the physician reported to you, you will become what it says. However, if you meditate on God's Word, you will become like a tree planted by rivers of living waters that brings forth fruitful health in season.

But his delight is in the law of the LORD, and in His law he meditates day and night. He shall be like a tree planted by the rivers of water, that brings forth its fruit in its season, whose leaf also shall not wither; and whatever he does shall prosper. (Psalm 1:2–3)

29

Mind Science or the Mind of Christ

The area of the mind and thoughts can be a touchy subject among evangelical Christians. Many Christians today seem to be so overly concerned about the possibility of being identified with anything related to New Age or mind science—which is generally defined as the exercise of human mental power independent from God—that they have cut themselves off from the truth of God's Word. What these Christians fail to realize is that much of the principles of mind science have been stolen from the Holy Scriptures and twisted to fit personal and sectarian applications. In the attempt to distinguish themselves as Bible-believing, holy, pious, theologically precise believers, many Christians have stripped the power of God out of the Bible. They have, in effect, crippled God by undermining and denying His power.

However, it must be maintained that there is one God who is supreme. He is not a science or a system. God is omnipotent, or infinite, in power. God is a God of miracles and a God of healing. God exists in a perpetual state of wholeness. Divine health should also be the perpetual state of the believing Christian.

The Scriptures tell us, *"We have the mind of Christ"* (1 Corinthians 2:16). If Christians have the mind of Christ, then we have in us everything that we will ever need to bring healing to our bodies.

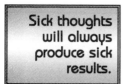
Sick thoughts will always produce sick results.

In order to receive our healing, we must first view our thoughts as being sick. Sick thoughts will always produce sick results. It is a sick thought to believe that God would create beings who are doomed with terminal sickness, disease, and premature death, but not provide a way of escape. What kind of God would that be? We need to get rid of thoughts like this.

Once our thoughts are healed, then our physical bodies will follow suit. We must be fully persuaded of God's will for His children. We also must be cautious not to weaken or deny God's power in us, just to please a group of so-called "heresy hunters" who will never be pleased. In fact, many of the people who attack power-filled ministries—those who demonstrate the power of Christ today and manifest the works of God to others—hold to a position that is antithetical to Scripture. They have *"a form of godliness but* [deny] *its power"* (2 Timothy 3:5). We are warned in this verse that we ought to *"turn away"* from *"such people."* Stay away from anyone who denies the power of God. God cannot be separated from His power. Begin to change your thoughts, focus on the fact that it is God's will to heal you, and you will change your health.

Your Remedy Is in the Word

The cure for every problem that life presents is found in two places. The first place we can find the cure is in God's Word. His Word thoroughly deals with anything that we may encounter. Every Scripture has been given to us to cause profit to come into our lives.

> *All Scripture is given by inspiration of God, and is profitable for doctrine, for reproof, for correction, for instruction in righteousness.* (2 Timothy 3:16)

31

For whatever things were written before were written for our learning, that we through the patience and comfort of the Scriptures might have hope. (Romans 15:4)

When the Word of the Lord was written, our solace was in the mind of the Father. God gives us hope through His Word. Several times I have heard people criticize faith ministries for giving "false hope" to those who are suffering with critical illnesses. In the natural realm, it may seem hopeless that some people will ever be healed. Nevertheless, our hope is not in man but in the Lord. As long as ministries direct people to God's Word, there can never be such a thing as a faith ministry giving people false hope. There are no false hopes in Jesus. In fact, He is our only hope.

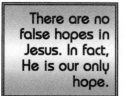

There are no false hopes in Jesus. In fact, He is our only hope.

Some say, "Just let him die in peace. Don't trouble him anymore. Let him spend his last days with his family, reminiscing over the precious moments they have shared." While that may sound good, it is totally unscriptural.

I would rather die believing that God would heal me than die not believing. As long as I have a destiny to fulfill in my life, I am going to fight. If I die, then I will die in faith. The promise of healing then becomes secondary to my pleasing God. *"Without faith it is impossible to please Him"* (Hebrews 11:6). I would much rather receive the prize than the promise. The prize is always greater than the promise.

These all died in faith, not having received the promises, but having seen them afar off were assured of them, embraced them and confessed that they were strangers and pilgrims on the earth. (Hebrews 11:13)

These heroes of the faith never received the fulfillment of the promise, yet they died believing. This does not suggest false hope but rather the highest spiritual attainment possible. They received the prize of the higher calling that is in Christ Jesus. The apostle Paul declared, *"I press toward the goal for the prize of the upward call of God in Christ Jesus"* (Philippians 3:14). This is the pinnacle of our faith.

The second place we can find the cure for life's problems is in ourselves, if we are believers. The cure for AIDS lies within us. The cure for cancer is lying dormant in some Christian believer. Not only do we have the solutions for peace and prosperity in us, but we *are* the solution. David understood that it was God's Word in him that caused him to resist the sinful nature. *"Your word I have hidden in my heart, that I might not sin against You!"* (Psalm 119:11). God's Word dwelled inside David. It's not the Word alone that produces results, but rather it is the Word of God in us.

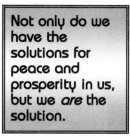

> Not only do we have the solutions for peace and prosperity in us, but we *are* the solution.

The Nature of the Kingdom

The kingdom of God is the rule and reign of the Lord Jesus Christ. He desires to establish His kingly order in the life of every believer. In this kingdom there is no lack, no sickness, no suffering. Jesus declared that all of the substance of the kingdom is inside us.

Now when He was asked by the Pharisees when the kingdom of God would come, He answered them and said, "The kingdom of God does not come with observation; nor will they say, 'See here!' or 'See there!' For indeed, the kingdom of God is within you."
(Luke 17:20–21)

Everything you will ever need in order to accomplish the will of God for your life lies within you in seed form. Your healing is in you in the form of a seed. That seed is called the Word. Once you tap into the seed of the kingdom that lives inside you, you will receive total wholeness, complete restoration, divine health, and kingdom fulfillment.

> Everything you will ever need in order to accomplish the will of God for your life lies within you in seed form.

For the kingdom of God is not eating and drinking, but righteousness and peace and joy in the Holy Spirit. (Romans 14:17)

The Word of God is the missing healing component. Once you have a revelation of God's Word and it becomes real to you, and real in you, your healing will be attained. God's Word declares that His ultimate desire is for you to walk in good health. Let God's Word become more real to you than life itself. Allow His Word to heal you now.

He sent His word and healed them, and delivered them from their destructions.
(Psalm 107:20)

chapter two

It's a Matter of Flesh and Blood

Your healing is an urgent matter to God. While there may be many who take healing and walking in divine health lightly, God does not. Recognize that God is an extremist, and He will always go to the most extreme measure to fulfill His divine promises, plans, and destiny for your life.

Let's examine just how serious God is about your healing. Notice I said, "how serious God *is*." God always is. His Word is always now.

Isaiah declared of Christ,

> *Surely He has borne our griefs and carried our sorrows; yet we esteemed Him stricken, smitten by God, and afflicted. But He was wounded for our transgressions, He was bruised for our iniquities; the chastisement for our peace was upon Him, and by His stripes we are healed.*
> (Isaiah 53:4–5)

Notice that Isaiah said, *"We are healed."* God operates so much in the present tense that even our healing is *now*.

Let's look further into passages in the Bible to see that divine healing is prophesied as coming through Christ's Atonement.

What Is Atonement?

In order for us to understand the atoning work of the Lord Jesus Christ, we must understand the meaning of the word *atonement*. The word *atonement* comes from the Hebrew word *kaphar*. *Kaphar* literally means "to cover." It means "to make reconciliation; to pacify or appease; to clear, purge, or cleanse; to disannul, cancel, or pardon." Atonement is the Christian teaching that the reconciliation of God and humankind has been accomplished through Christ's blood sacrifice. In this blood sacrifice, full provision for salvation for the spirit and soul is made possible. An equal provision for total healing is also granted in this blood sacrifice.

In Hebrew tradition, the Day of Atonement is the tenth day of the month of Tishrei. This Jewish holy day is called Yom Kippur. Although the Torah does not say it, this day is thought to be the holiest day of the Jewish year. Perhaps this day is revered with such high regard because on this day the high priest was allowed to enter the Holy of Holies in the temple. Today on Yom Kippur, Jewish people spend the entire day fasting and praying to the Lord for forgiveness. They believe that during this one day, if they repent, their sins will be forgiven.

> **forgive**: to grant pardon for or remission of an offense or sin; to absolve or to cancel or to remit a debt or a claim against; to grant relief from payment of a debt or an obligation.

When one's sins are atoned for, the high price of sin is paid in full by the one whose blood is sacrificed. Under the old covenant, the blood of animals was used as a substitutionary sacrifice for sins. Under the new covenant, the blood of animals would not suffice to redeem us from sin and bring us back to God the Father. In order for humanity to be reconnected to God, it would take a human sacrifice. It would take a pure and sinless sacrifice. It would take the blood of the Lord Jesus Christ.

> *For if the blood of bulls and goats and the ashes of a heifer, sprinkling the unclean, sanctifies for the purifying of the flesh, how much more shall the blood of Christ, who through the eternal Spirit offered Himself without spot to God, cleanse your conscience from dead works to serve the living God? And for this reason He is the Mediator of the new covenant, by means of death, for the redemption of the transgressions under the first covenant, that those who are called may receive the promise of the eternal inheritance.*
> (Hebrews 9:13–15)

The Lord Jesus became our Atonement, our covering for sin. He covered our sin. Jesus did not hide our sins; He covered them with His blood. There is a distinct difference between hiding something and covering something. Sin is great in its effect on the soul and cannot be hidden. But it can be covered by something of a greater magnitude. That is where the blood of Jesus comes in.

Once the pure blood of Jesus touches our sin, the sin becomes suffocated by the overwhelming presence of God's love. Then we are purged and cleansed in the sight of God. Through this purging and cleansing process, our debt for sin is cleared, making us free from all spiritual debt. This appeases and satisfies God, bringing us back into fellowship with Him forever. This process is called atonement.

Through this process we can be in a state of oneness with God, or at-one-ment. We must always recognize that we could never be one with God or in right relationship with Him without the sacrifice of the Lord Jesus. It is totally in Christ that we have our redemption and have received forgiveness for our sin and iniquity.

> *In Him we have redemption through His blood, the forgiveness of sins, according to the riches of His grace.* (Ephesians 1:7)

Many of us have accepted the reality of Christ's blood as the Atonement for our sins. Rarely have we accepted the same sacrifice to suffice for our healing. We have failed to recognize that the same blood that Jesus shed, which was powerful enough to remit sin, has power to remit sickness and disease.

> *And according to the law almost all things are purified with blood, and without shedding of blood there is no remission.*
> (Hebrews 9:22)

Life Is in the Blood

Under the old covenant only blood could atone for souls, for in the blood is life.

> *For the life of the flesh is in the blood, and I have given it to you upon the altar to make atonement for your souls; for it is*

> *the blood that makes atonement for the soul.* (Leviticus 17:11)

The truth that life is in the blood is very interesting. Blood is the vital principle of life. Blood is the fluid of life, transporting oxygen from the lungs to body tissue and carbon dioxide from body tissue to the lungs. Blood is the fluid of growth and development, transporting nourishment from glands throughout the entire body. Blood is the fluid of health, transporting disease-fighting substances to tissue and waste to the kidneys. Blood contains living cells. Because cells are alive, blood is alive.

There is no wonder why blood had to be offered for us by Jesus. Through the sacrifice of His blood, we regained life, and that *"more abundantly"* (John 10:10). Anyone who does not enjoy the benefits of this abundant life is being miserably robbed by the thief called religion, which comes to steal the Word and leaves its victims to die in the abyss of ignorance.

> *The thief does not come except to steal, and to kill, and to destroy. I have come that they may have life, and that they may have it more abundantly.* (John 10:10)

Sin, Sickness, and Death

Sickness is sin. That statement generally arouses great contempt in people. Their reaction underscores great misunderstanding and ignorance. They become defensive when they hear that statement because it seems to imply that sickness and disease overcome us because we are participating in some heinous sin. Please understand that your personal sin will not produce the profusion of sickness and diseases that plague the world.

Your personal sin will affect you personally, and it can also affect your offspring in both natural and spiritual ways. In fact, God will punish the sins of the fathers as far back as four generations when there is no repentance.

> *The LORD is longsuffering and abundant in mercy, forgiving iniquity and transgression; but He by no means clears the guilty, visiting the iniquity of the fathers on the children to the third and fourth generation.*
> (Numbers 14:18)

However, original sickness, like original sin, is the result of one man. That one man's sin brought sin- and sickness-consciousness on all of humanity. Sickness is the result of original sin in Adam. The Bible declares,

> *Through one man sin entered the world, and death through sin, and thus death spread to all men, because all sinned.*
> (Romans 5:12)

Through one man, sin and death entered the world. What is death? Death is the cessation of spiritual or natural life. Therefore anything that hinders the healthy flow of life is the enemy of life, slowly ushering in death. Furthermore, anything that prevents the progression of life is also an enemy of God. With that understanding, sickness in any form is embryonic death. Sickness is death.

One act of one man brought sin and its penalty of death and sickness upon the entire human race. Conversely, one act of one Man brought righteousness and its reward of life, which includes divine health now and eternal life in ages to come, upon the entire human race. Adam led old humanity, marked by sin, sickness, and death. Jesus leads new humanity, typified by righteousness, divine health, and eternal life. We inherit the consequences of Adam's disobedience and faithlessness by being naturally born into this world. We inherit the blessing associated with Christ's obedience by being born again.

The father of the sin nature and sickness nature is the devil, who introduced them by getting Adam to taste their fruit. Both sin and sickness have the same lineage. They are both offspring of the devil. Thus, they bear the same last name, death.

Removing the Unclean Thing

The source of sin and sickness is evil, which makes both sin and sickness intrinsically evil as well. Once we begin to view sickness as evil, we will no longer welcome its residence in our bodies. When we begin to view sickness as unclean, we will serve sickness an eviction notice. No unclean thing should dwell in our mortal bodies.

> Or do you not know that your body is the temple of the Holy Spirit who is in you, whom you have from God, and you are not your own? For you were bought at a price; therefore glorify God in your body and in your spirit, which are God's.
> (1 Corinthians 6:19–20)

Many have thought of this Scripture as dealing solely with sexual immorality because the

...evious verses expound on sexual sins. However, our physical bodies can be defiled by more than sexual immorality. Yes, our bodies can be defiled or made unclean by sickness and disease. The last part of verse twenty deals with glorifying God in our bodies and also our spirits. Your physical body can give glory and honor to God when it is in good health. Just as your spirit man requires freedom from anything that would defile it, so your physical body needs to be free of sickness and disease. Sickness and disease can only hinder you from fulfilling your God-given destiny.

> Sickness and disease can only hinder you from fulfilling your God-given destiny.

Let's look at a Bible passage that deals with what is unclean in relation to physical sickness.

> *And the LORD spoke to Moses and Aaron, saying: "When a man has on the skin of his body a swelling, a scab, or a bright spot, and it becomes on the skin of his body like a leprous sore, then he shall be brought to Aaron the priest or to one of his sons the priests. The priest shall examine the sore on the skin of the body; and if the hair on the sore has turned white, and the sore appears to be deeper than the skin of his body, it is a leprous sore. Then the priest shall examine him, and pronounce him unclean.* (Leviticus 13:1–3)

Under the old covenant, a leprous or disfigured sick person was called *"unclean,"* which means defiled. A sick person was considered defiled. The patient would have to be examined by the priest, whose job included administering health care to the sick and diseased.

In the seventeenth chapter of Luke, we find the story of the ten lepers who were cleansed by Jesus. These ten men who needed cleansing lifted up their voices, crying out to Jesus to have mercy on them. Jesus spoke these words: *"Go, show yourselves to the priests,"* and as they were obeying the instruction from the Lord, *"they were cleansed"* (Luke 17:14).

Being healed, they were now able to give glory to God the way they were originally intended to as whole, complete beings. Prior to receiving their healing, they could not give full glory or honor to God. Physical sickness hinders us from giving total praise and worship to God with all of our being.

> *And one of them, when he saw that he was healed, returned, and with a loud voice glorified God, and fell down on his face at His feet, giving Him thanks. And he was a Samaritan.* (Luke 17:15–16)

After he was healed, not before, the Samaritan gave thanks and glorified the Lord. Before he could give full and proper allegiance to God, he first had to have the unclean thing removed from him. Jesus inquired, *"Were there not any found who returned to give glory to God except this foreigner?"* (verse 18). Jesus recognized that there were ten people who were eligible to give honor and glory to God, yet only one did so.

For many years, I have noticed a negative trait in some people after Jesus has healed them. Time after time I have heard people swear that if God would heal them and deliver them from sickness, they would be faithful to Him for the rest of their lives. They promise that they would attend church regularly and support the local church with tithes and offerings. How sad it is that many of these same people, when healed, never come to worship and give God glory. They never come to church to give thanks to the Lord. They never honor the Lord with the firstfruits of their increase, their tithes and offerings. They never bring glory to the Father for His marvelous work. When God heals us, it is for His glory, not ours. An attitude of ingratitude toward Jesus now will prevent future occasions of fellowshipping with Him.

God wants to remove the unclean thing, sickness, from us so that our service will be of maximum benefit to Him. You must view sickness as unclean and unacceptable in your body. I am not suggesting that because you are sick you are unclean, but rather that you carry or house something that is unclean and defiled. You are and will always be precious in the sight of God.

However, you are to view sickness with the same attitude that God has toward sickness. God looks at sickness as the result of sin and sin-consciousness. There is only one cure for sin. The blood of Jesus is sin's only remedy. Accepting the Lord's sacrifice on the cross and the blood that He shed frees us from sin's influence over our lives. The same is required to eliminate sickness from our lives forever. Accepting the Lord's sacrifice on the cross and the blood that He shed frees us from the influence that sickness has over our lives.

Discerning the Body of the Lord

Although we will address in detail the topic of Holy Communion in a later chapter, it is appropriate to deal with the relationship of the Lord's body to sickness and healing at this time.

The Bible informs us that when we partake of the sacrament of Holy Communion, or the Eucharist, we partake of the Lord's body. The Bible declares,

> *And when He had given thanks, He broke it and said, "Take, eat; this is My body which is broken for you; do this in remembrance of Me."* (1 Corinthians 11:24)

The *"body which is broken for you"* refers to our Lord's role as Savior and also as the One who bore our pain and sicknesses. (See Isaiah 53:4–6.) The bread served in Communion represents the broken body of Jesus. This is why we break the bread before serving Communion. When we break bread, it typifies how our Savior willingly gave His body to be broken for us.

> *And as they were eating, Jesus took bread, blessed and broke it, and gave it to the disciples and said, "Take, eat; this is My body."* (Matthew 26:26)

In First Corinthians, the apostle Paul turned the focus of Communion to self-examination, which includes *"discerning the Lord's body"*:

> *But let a man examine himself, and so let him eat of the bread and drink of the cup. For he who eats and drinks in an unworthy manner eats and drinks judgment to himself, not discerning the Lord's body. For this reason many are weak and sick among you, and many sleep. For if we would judge ourselves, we would not be judged.* (1 Corinthians 11:28–31)

These Scriptures deal in a strict way with the person who refuses to judge himself and who does not properly discern the body of Christ. The phrase *"the Lord's body"* can refer to His spiritual body, known as the church or the congregation. To drink *"in an unworthy manner"* could constitute drinking the cup of the Lord while denying the power and presence of God in another or unfamiliar part of the body of Christ.

I believe that many who feel it is their responsibility to be watchdogs, heresy hunters, and critics of ministries fall directly into this category of those who drink *"in an unworthy manner."* They believe that the body of Christ consists only of those whom *they* say are acceptable. They believe that the body of Christ should worship and praise God only in the way *they* worship and praise Him. They believe that the body of Christ is confined to a particular denomination or movement or ethnic group. If you don't meet all of their requirements, they exclude you from the body with their words.

You may have heard members of a church say, "Anyone who is not part of my church is surely bound for hell." This kind of arrogant exclusion will cause weakness, sickness, and in some cases premature death to come upon members of that congregation. This kind of judgment will certainly keep God's healing presence away from that church!

In addition, continual, habitual judgment of others will disqualify you from the body of Christ, because you cannot love God and hate your brothers simultaneously. (See 1 John 4:20.) Chronic judging turns your focus from your relationship with Christ and distracts you from your real purpose, which is to preach Christ and His kingdom.

God takes it very seriously when we self-righteously examine others and declare them as being unworthy to be Christians. He takes it very seriously when we judge others' ministry gifts. Judgmental people bring great disappointment to God, because they not only hinder the progress of the kingdom, but they also try to sit in the seat that is clearly marked, "RESERVED FOR THE KING."

Judgment causes great harm to the body of Christ. It causes division and strife among people whom God intended to be united under one head, Christ. When we separate ourselves from one another because of our judgment, it's counterproductive to the one, united body that God desires.

There are some things that the Lord takes personally. One of those things is His body. Jesus gave His physical body to be crucified for us. His flesh was ripped and torn. *"He was wounded for our transgressions"* (Isaiah 53:5). He shed His blood for the remission of sin and sickness. Now, because of the oneness we as believers have with Christ through the forgiveness and regeneration His sacrifice brought, He refers to us as His very own body.

Thus, when we come to the table of the Lord, we must recognize His sacrifice and our unity in Christ with other believers. We must recognize how wonderfully different the people are for whom He was broken. We disqualify ourselves from His body when we attempt to disqualify other Christians from His body. Satan is *"the accuser of our brethren"* (Revelation 12:10); it is not our job as the people of God to accuse our fellow believers. We can condemn sin, but we don't have the right to judge the sinner. The personal cost of such judgment is too high a price to pay.

Judge not, that you be not judged.
(Matthew 7:1)

> *Therefore you are inexcusable, O man, whoever you are who judge, for in whatever you judge another you condemn yourself; for you who judge practice the same things.* (Romans 2:1)

Healing Is Who God Is

Now let's consider the names and nature of God. We have covered the subject of atonement as it relates to forgiveness, redemption, and restoration. We need now to look at redemption, not in the light of what God does, but in the light of who He is in redemption.

God has many names. We need to know that His names are directly connected to who He is and are indicative of His intrinsic redemptive nature. Here is a list of some of the names of God with correlating Scripture references.

Yahweh-Yatsar   *The Lord Our Creator*
Genesis 2:7–8, 19
Yahweh-Gaal   *The Lord Our Redeemer*
Isaiah 44:24
Yahweh-Shalom   *The Lord Our Peace*
Judges 6:24
Yahweh-Raah   *The Lord Our Shepherd*
Psalm 23:1
Yahweh-Jireh   *The Lord Our Provider*
Genesis 22:14
Yahweh-Nasa   *The Lord Our Sin-Bearer*
Exodus 34:6–7   *& Forgiver*
Yahweh-Tsidkenu   *The Lord Our Righteousness*
Jeremiah 23:6
Yahweh-Rapha   *The Lord Our Healer*
Exodus 15:26

As we look at this partial listing of God's names, we must realize that each one of these represents who God is, not merely what He does. For example, Yahweh-Shalom describes God as One who brings peace. Better still is knowing that God *is* peace. He does not just forgive; He *is* forgiveness. God does not only provide; He *is* provision. His names reveal far more than what He does. His redemptive names reveal who He is. Who God is *is* the nature of His character.

A Rose by Any Other Name

Let us consider the following illustration. Many of you married women remember when your husband-to-be was courting you. Although it may have been long ago, it seems like yesterday when he brought you a dozen long-stemmed red roses. Every other week he bought your favorite Godiva chocolates. Even during the initial months after the wedding, he prepared a first-class dinner by candlelight just to show how much he loved you. You both enjoyed the lengthy walks through the park as you held hands and shared intimate secrets. How sweet those memories are!

Now times are different. It has been years since you've seen a flower or a box of chocolates from him. The closest thing to a first-class dinner now is a Hungry Man meal, fresh from the microwave. He's usually so tired when he arrives home from work that you no longer take walks. The intimate secrets have been replaced by arguing over the bills and the kids' schooling. If only the good old days would return!

The primary reason a man does not continue to do what he did in the past is that it was not in his nature to begin with. If it were ingrained in his character, he could never completely stop doing it.

God cannot do what His names connote and then stop. He has to continually do what His names indicate because they represent who He is.

Suppose a doctor is away from home on vacation with his wife and children. If someone where he is vacationing has a heart attack, he will administer medical treatment to that person. Why? He is a doctor. His profession goes beyond what he does at the hospital to make a living. It is who he is. If a doctor can see a person dying and not give help, then he is not a genuine doctor but rather a hireling—he is only in the profession for the money, not the people. What you are is what you do. What you do represents who you are.

One of the redemptive names of God is Yahweh-Rapha, which means "the Lord our Healer" or "the Great Physician." The Bible declares,

> *If you diligently heed the voice of the LORD your God and do what is right in His sight, give ear to His commandments and keep all His statutes, I will put none of the diseases on you which I have brought on the Egyptians. For I am the LORD who heals you.* (Exodus 15:26)

The psalmist declared,

> *Bless the LORD, O my soul, and forget not all His benefits: who forgives all your iniquities, who heals all your diseases.* (Psalm 103:2–3)

Yahweh-Rapha is one of God's names. His appellations don't center on what He does; instead, they always focus on who He is. Not only does God heal, but also God is healing. He is healing personified. He cannot be anything to a sick and diseased person other than healing, because that is who He is. God is not like the husband who used to do lovely things for his wife but no longer does. For God to cease from healing, He would have to cease being God.

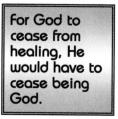

For God to cease from healing, He would have to cease being God.

Contrary to popular belief, God does not heal occasionally or sometimes. For God to heal every now and then would invalidate the redemptive power of His name, Yahweh-Rapha, the Great Physician. He is always the Healer. His healing power is infinite. God is in a perpetual state of divine health. Quite naturally, God never gets sick. He is not diseased. His constant state of health and wholeness is for you and me also. Once we recognize that He is healing, we have won more than half the battle.

The Resident, Indwelling God

The other part of the mental battle deals with knowing where God lives in relationship to His children.

You are of God, little children, and have overcome them, because He who is in you is greater than he who is in the world.
(1 John 4:4)

To them God willed to make known what are the riches of the glory of this mystery among the Gentiles: which is Christ in you, the hope of glory. (Colossians 1:27)

Do you not know that you are the temple of God and that the Spirit of God dwells in you? (1 Corinthians 3:16)

We know from this Scripture where the Spirit of God resides. God lives in you. It is absolutely amazing to realize that the almighty God of the universe lives inside you. Even more wonderful is that all of His nature and character are also in you. All that God is dwells inside you. Just based on our brief list of God's redemptive names, you can see that unlimited amounts of creative power, leadership, provision, forgiveness, peace, righteousness, and healing are resident within you.

> It is absolutely amazing to realize that the almighty God of the universe lives inside you.

However, all of the qualities and attributes of God are like untapped energy in you. The potential for your healing is already inside you. The more you focus on the reality of Christ in you, the more you will walk in the reality of who God is. On the contrary, the more you focus on the limitations of the physical realm, the more you will discount and disconnect your divine connection to God.

Healing is a matter of flesh and blood. We don't have to make the way, nor do we have to fight to attain our healing. When Jesus shed His blood, when His flesh was torn, and when He was resurrected from the grave, your victory was won. There is no need to fight. He has already won the war for you, and one of the battles He won was for your healing.

Discover your healing, for it is already within you.

chapter three

Now Faith

Everything in the kingdom of God is appropriated through the spiritual mechanism we know as faith. Absolutely nothing works in the kingdom of God without faith's application and process. Nothing good happens to you "just because." We must live in a mode of constant faith in order to realize the lifestyle God intended us to enjoy.

The message of faith has often been distorted or erroneously taught over the centuries. Many have read into the message of faith and thus misinterpreted it. Over the years there have been extremes on both ends of the faith spectrum. One extreme denies the power of God, the miraculous, and the rewards of living in continual abundance in every area of life. The opposite position attributes faith to that which is spiritually presumptuous—almost expecting God to be at our beck and call. Both of these excesses are equally dangerous and unproductive.

What we desperately need is true balance. The faith balance is never equalized by adding proportionate doses of unbelief or presumption, but rather by having a thorough understanding of the meaning of faith, how it operates, and what faith is not. This is the balance that millions seek to possess, yet they often fall prey to the extremes on either side of faith as they seek the central point of balance. Unfortunately, these extremes never produce healthy results, but rather frustration, guilt, embarrassment, and chagrin.

It is my desire to unfold the true nature of faith to you. But beyond its revelation to you, I pray that you will receive God's best in this learning experience. God's best is not His revelation *to* you, but rather His revelation *in* you.

Faith Is a Simple Matter

One of the things that can be so frustrating for believers is when they complicate a simple theme. God's Word and the themes in His Word were written to be easily understood. Some theologians have earned their B.D. in philosophy— their "Beyond Divinity" degree—thus elevating their personal statements of philosophical reasoning above the supremacy of God. Furthermore, their personal reasoning is almost impossible for the common mind to comprehend.

Complicating what God's Word says about faith makes the devil rejoice. The enemy knows better than most Christians that without faith it is impossible to bring pleasure to God.

> *But without faith it is impossible to please Him, for he who comes to God must believe that He is, and that He is a rewarder of those who diligently seek Him.*
> (Hebrews 11:6)

Using simple logic, we can see that when God is not getting any pleasure, quite naturally the devil is. The enemy has made it his full-time career to keep believers ignorant of their covenant rights. He majors in keeping believers ignorant of faith's everyday operations. But the veil of ignorance will be lifted from this day forward for you.

What Is Faith?

There are many definitions of faith. Let's look at some facets of faith from various perspectives.

> **faith**: confidence or trust in a person or thing; belief that is not based on proof; belief in God or in the doctrines or teachings of religion; belief in anything, as a code of ethics or standards of merit.

These common dictionary definitions have intertwined strands that are strikingly similar. The similarity has to do with the fact that many people make a false connection between faith and belief. Although these concepts are similar, they are not the same. A Rolls Royce and a Bentley are similar, but they are not the same. They do not have the same shape. They do not cost the same amount. They are no longer manufactured by the same people. Yet they appear to be the same. Only a Rolls Royce or a Bentley enthusiast would immediately recognize the distinctions between the two.

Faith and belief are not the same, although the majority of people think they are. To be ignorant of the differences between faith and belief can cost us far more than we are willing to pay.

People often think that because they have a strong belief in something, their belief qualifies as faith. You can believe in God and yet not have faith in God. If you ask most people if they believe in God, more than likely they will answer with a resounding yes. Most individuals do believe in a

Supreme Being, but that doesn't mean they have faith in God.

Well, what is the difference? In order to have genuine faith in God, you must believe God, not merely believe *in* Him. There is a great difference between believing *in* God and believing God. To believe in God simply means that you believe that God exists. You believe that God is presently manifesting Himself as the preeminent One. You acknowledge that He is the power behind the force of creation. You agree that God represents the universal superglue that holds everything in the cosmos firmly together.

My real concern is this: Do you really believe

Do you really believe God? ...Do you believe that His power dwells in you and is omnipotent?

God? Do you believe every word that He said as it is recorded in the Bible? Do you believe that His power dwells in you and is omnipotent? Do you believe that God has placed in your spirit a boundless, unrestricted, limitless nature? Do you believe that God is speaking to you right now? Do you believe that according to God's Word you possess your healing right now? Do you believe that God is working miracles and mighty works in the earthly realm? Do you believe that in performing miracles and mighty works He can operate through a willing candidate, possibly you?

If you answered yes to all of these questions, then it is likely that you believe God. If you answered no to any of these questions, perhaps you believe in God, but you do not believe God. Real faith begins with believing God.

Various dictionaries define the word *faith* as having belief that is not based on proof. This is how the unspiritual person usually defines faith. However, the spiritual believer knows that beyond any doubt, our faith is backed by strong proof— God's Word. God's Word is our evidence. Whatever He says, it is already done and performed.

You might be asking, "Then why don't I see the full manifestation of my faith? Why don't I see the material proof?" The answer is that you have not yet discovered or realized the source of attaining what you have been believing for. What you desire is already in you. However, what is in you needs to come out of you to bring the maximum benefit to you.

> What is in you needs to come out of you to bring the maximum benefit to you.

Untapped potential is meaningless. Latent energy is powerless. If you never plug the lamp into the outlet, you will never receive the current from the electrical plant to power the lamp. If you never make a withdrawal from your savings account or investments, you will never receive the use and benefits of the money. The potential is there, but you have not tapped into it yet because you have belief but have not yet entered into faith.

Your healing becomes a manifested reality when your faith makes a demand on your physical body to perform as God declares it should. Thus, your *act* of believing God overrides any possible thought that goes against what God has said. The doctor's diagnosis and prognosis then become trivial to your soul because your soul has already been prospered by what God has spoken.

If I were to compose songs and write books declaring that Bill Gates, the president of the Microsoft Corporation, was living in abject poverty, it would be a pointless pursuit. Why? Mr. Gates has plenty of evidence to substantiate his present status and affluence. Because his soul has prospered beyond all of his peers in the area of business knowledge and success, his mind cannot downshift to a lesser degree of power. His level of contribution to society has been, without question, one of excellence. He has reached this level by realizing who he is in relation to the business world and as one of the foremost technological prophets of our modern-day era.

Bill Gates has made a discovery of what he believes he deserves. Now he is acting on his belief system. Because he has received this revelation of who he is in the business world, he does not receive any undercutting remarks about himself, since they do not represent this higher level of thought and self-perception. He is a billionaire, not because he strives to be, but rather because that is who he is. Microsoft Corporation is the leading computer software company in the world, not solely because of its quality product line, but rather because of the mind of its founder. His mind realizes that Microsoft is the world leader of software products. Nothing less than this realization is acceptable.

What have you allowed to become acceptable in your life? Does God's Word speak louder than the glut of negative words that you hear in everyday society? If you allow any word to have more influence over you than the authenticity of God's Word does, you have allowed something unacceptable to transpire in your spirit. You have compromised your faith and distorted its meaning. Finally, you have aborted any possibility of attaining healing and wholeness.

Believing God is the very basic foundation of real faith. Simply stated, faith is believing God. The most elementary thing that God desires us to do is just believe Him.

> *Jesus said to him, "If you can believe, all things are possible to him who believes."*
> (Mark 9:23)

Faith Is *Now*

> *Now faith is the substance of things hoped for, the evidence of things not seen.*
> (Hebrews 11:1)

As we discover the reality of faith, we find another truth concerning it: Faith is *now*. Faith never *will be,* and faith never *was.* Faith is always today and will never be tomorrow. It is paramount that you understand and accept this truth concerning the "nowness" of faith. The reason this understanding is so crucial is that any other kind of faith is deceptive, fraudulent, and phony.

It would be tragic to live life believing that you had something genuine, only to discover that it was a fake. Yesterday's faith is not faith at all. You do not have to believe for something that already exists in your life. Once you receive what you have been believing for, you have what is called a manifestation. Once you have the manifested result, you no longer need faith for that.

For example, suppose you desire healing in your physical body or in your emotions. One day it dawns on you—you discover your true self. You know that you are saved. You realize that you have been born again. You recognize that you were transformed, or re-created, because the old you did not think properly. Now you think like God thinks. You have the mind of Christ. You receive the healing that Christ has made possible for you to enjoy. Your faith has appropriated your healing to you in the physical realm. You used your faith. Once you have received your healing, though, you can no longer consider it to be in the realm of faith. In other words, it would be improper to consider you a person of faith in relation to this particular healing.

Men and women of faith are perpetually exercising their faith with every opportunity that arises. Faith that has received its reward is not the same thing as faith. It is like a caterpillar awaiting its transformation into a beautiful butterfly. Once the caterpillar becomes a butterfly, it can no longer be labeled a caterpillar. Have you ever heard someone say of a butterfly, "That's the most beautiful caterpillar I have ever seen"? How absurd! It would be just as absurd to say that a person is a person of faith solely because he has used his faith once or twice in the past. Faith is always *now*.

In addition, faith is never in the future. Many of us have been guilty of saying, "I am believing God for this or that in the future." This sounds very religious, but it irritates God a great deal. The reason this aggravates God so much is that we limit God's potential in us by putting our faith into the future. God wants you to be blessed *now*. God wants you to receive healing *now*. God desires you to walk in prosperity *now*. Your harvest is *now*.

Future faith is not faith at all; it is an enemy of faith. This enemy is also called "hope." Biblical hope is not an enemy, for we see many scriptural applications of genuine hope that confirm its validity. However, many people embrace a type of hope that is an enemy of faith. This hope puts off until tomorrow what we can receive by faith today. It says, "Someday I'll be healed," "Money will come to me someday," and, "One day I'll have healthy relationships." Hope always puts off the present for the future. Hope creates an environment that would seem to produce manifested results, yet nothing is ever really seen. Hope is illusory, while faith is real.

Why is this important? The nature of faith reflects the nature of God. Please understand that God is an eternal being. He exists in eternity.

> *"I am the Alpha and the Omega, the Beginning and the End," says the Lord, "who is and who was and who is to come, the Almighty."* (Revelation 1:8)

God is the beginning and the end of everything that we can see with our natural eyes. God had to begin the beginning for us. He also will bring the last chapter of the earthly existence of humanity as we know it to an end. God has al-

God is the beginning and the end of everything that we can see with our natural eyes. God had to begin the beginning for us.

ways existed in eternity, which means He has no beginning or ending.

God created time for mortal man. Time helps us to mark our progress as we march toward the fulfillment of our destiny. However, God is an eternal spirit and is not limited by anything. He is not charted by or confined to time. This means that everything in God is now. When God wants to accomplish His purpose in a person, He will wait for hundreds of generations for that one person who will say yes. God never wants to hear, "Lord, You can use me in a few years." Such talk is foolishness in God's ears. Your body may be totally riddled with disease, and God has vowed to heal you, yet you say, "Not now, God." God won't force you to take His gift of healing, so He will find someone else through whom He can manifest His healing power. Faith is *now!*

God, like faith, never will be, but is. He lives in the eternal *now*. God's limitless capacity is what He expects us to receive and to live by. We were created in the image of God.

> Then God said, "Let Us make man in Our image, according to Our likeness; let them have dominion over the fish of the sea, over the birds of the air, and over the cattle, over all the earth and over every creeping thing that creeps on the earth."
> (Genesis 1:26)

How are we created in the image and likeness of God? When we reflect God's eternal nature, we exemplify Him. When we recognize that all of His character is for our use here and now, and we begin to apply it, we then look like God.

Let us look again at the book of beginnings: *"Then God said, 'Let there be light'; and there was light"* (Genesis 1:3). When God said, *"Let there be light,"* light was. It happened in that *now* moment. Faith is not past, nor will it be in the future. Release your faith now, and receive what God has promised to give you. Receive your healing *now!*

Faith Is a Lifestyle

> For we walk by faith, not by sight.
> (2 Corinthians 5:7)

Faith is a lifestyle. Faith is not something that we do every now and then, but rather it is something that we live by every day. Faith is an operable system by which we govern our attitudes and perspectives on life. Our choices are based upon our faith. What we speak is based upon our faith. It is a confession of faith. For the Christian believer, faith is our creed. Faith determines our worldview. Faith is our map. It is how we navigate through this life. We cannot do anything or become anything in this life or the life to come apart from faith.

Faith is habitual, yet it is not legalistic. In other words, we do not have to meet a daily faith requirement in order to be justified or even pleasing in the sight of God. Faith is not like a set of rules that must be followed or else. Faith is as natural to the one who lives by it as bathing daily, brushing one's teeth, or combing one's hair. Faith is natural. It is not forced.

Although faith is habitual, it is not always rehearsed. There are many times when our faith will rise to the occasion for one special moment. This spontaneity causes us to give God all the glory for the victory that was won. Faith is like second nature. More than something we do, faith is something we are. We, the righteousness of God, are men and women of faith.

> *For in it the righteousness of God is revealed from faith to faith; as it is written, "The just shall live by faith."* (Romans 1:17)

The Bible chronicles great men and women of faith in Hebrews, chapter eleven. There we find a timely record of many who lived by faith. Note that the actual feats of faith that are recorded in this Scripture represent a zenith in the lives of these individuals who had been living a lifestyle of believing God.

Faith Is Progressive

Becoming a person who can move mountains does not usually happen overnight. You must begin to trust God *today* to move molehills. Faith is progressive. As we major in faith on its minor levels, we will qualify for greater adventures in faith on higher levels. Faith must be mastered first in its infant stages. This is crucial. Trying to operate on a level of faith without being qualified for it could cost our lives and ruin our destiny.

Abraham was seventy-five years old when the Lord told him to leave his country, his family, and his father's household. In our present culture, by that age, men have usually been retired from their careers for several years. In most cases they would not be thinking about becoming sojourners or relocating their places of residence.

However, God told Abraham to go. Abraham went, *"not knowing where he was going"* (Hebrews 11:8). The journey that Abraham undertook in his seasoned age was more than 1500 miles, but it was energized by faith. It was this early step of faith and obedience that prepared him to be willing to sacrifice his son Isaac unto the Lord. (See Genesis 22:1–18.)

Moses was also a man of faith. The Bible tells us,

> *By faith Moses, when he was born, was hidden three months by his parents, because they saw he was a beautiful child; and they were not afraid of the king's command.* (Hebrews 11:23)

In this Scripture, we see that Moses was blessed by his parents' act of faith, by their using him as the offering of faith. It was this act of faith that later set the stage for Moses to refuse to acknowledge Pharaoh's daughter as his mother. This personal act of faith, in turn, caused courage to rise when he was commissioned by God to tell Pharaoh, *"Let My people go"* (e.g., Exodus 8:1). The results of this subsequent act of faith then strengthened Moses to act in faith when the next occasion arose in which faith was needed, parting the Red Sea, and so on.

The central point here is that faith can be progressively developed. It becomes greater and more visible with each use. As we use our faith, it gives opportunities for greater levels of faith achievements. When we fail to use our faith in the simple things, we may eventually lose our faith. Although your faith may be small now, like the mustard seed it will become visible in due season.

The lifestyle of the rich in faith is always going from one stage to another stage to another stage. As you enter into a lifestyle of faith, you will not even think about the capacity of your faith because it will become familiar to you. Just as it is normal for you to inhale and exhale, it will be natural for you to live by faith.

Faith Is Action

My final consideration in this chapter deals with faith's activity. Faith is an action word. Faith is most respected as a moving, thriving, living thing. All of the facets of faith that have been discussed are useless if you do not catch hold of this reality. Faith is something that you have to use.

Faith does not just happen. You have to initiate faith by your action. After it has been initiated, it then becomes the responsibility of God to perform the work that has begun. Many people claim to believe the Bible yet do not act on what God's Word says. It is possible to hear the Word yet not do anything about the Word that you have heard.

> *But be doers of the word, and not hearers only, deceiving yourselves. For if anyone is a hearer of the word and not a doer, he is like a man observing his natural face in a mirror; for he observes himself, goes away, and immediately forgets what kind of man he was. But he who looks into the perfect law of liberty and continues in it, and is not a forgetful hearer but a doer of the work, this one will be blessed in what he does.* (James 1:22–25)

Throughout Scripture, we see many examples of faith in action. Abraham was told by God to sacrifice his son Isaac. Abraham began to put action to his faith by walking up the mountain to the place where the altar of sacrifice was. Before climbing the mountain, he split the wood that would be burned on the altar for the sacrifice. Abraham put his faith into action. (See Genesis 22:1–18.)

Jacob was another man who put his faith into action. By faith, Jacob wrestled with the angel of the Lord. He would not let go until he received an impartation from God. Jacob did something—he wrestled. God blessed Jacob and changed his name from Jacob to Israel. (See Genesis 32:24–28.)

In the fifth chapter of Luke, Jesus explained to Simon that if he wanted to catch a great mass of fish, he had to *do* something. The thing that was required was for Simon to let down his net in the deep water. Jesus said, *"Launch out into the deep"* (Luke 5:4). Just as one is often told to "think outside the box," Jesus wanted to adjust Simon's in-the-boat thinking. Simon explained to Jesus that he had fished all night yet had caught nothing. Jesus, who did not look to the circumstances, assured him that if he acted differently, he would receive differently. Although Simon did not fully comprehend, he obeyed. That day he caught more fish than he had ever caught. Simon put his faith into action.

In the ninth chapter of John, we read about Jesus healing a man who had been blind since birth. Before this man could get his healing, Jesus required the man to do something. He required him to participate in his healing process.

> *And He said to him, "Go, wash in the pool of Siloam" (which is translated, Sent). So he went and washed, and came back seeing.*   (John 9:7)

These are action words: *"So he went and washed."* The man did something, and he received something. A blind man put his faith into action and became a seeing man.

Mark 5:25–34 records the story of a woman who was cured of a hemorrhaging problem that had lasted for twelve years. This woman had spent all of her money going to physicians, yet her condition had only worsened. Out of desperation, she decided to do something. Although she was considered to be ceremonially unclean, she took the risk of faith. In biblical times, if a person who was bleeding was caught trying to touch someone in public, he or she could be immediately stoned to death. But this woman felt as if she were dying anyway, so it really did not matter to her; she had to try to touch Jesus.

> *When she heard about Jesus, she came behind Him in the crowd and touched His garment. For she said, "If only I may touch His clothes, I shall be made well."*
>
> (Mark 5:27–28)

She took a great risk, but her faith was rewarded. The woman with *"a flow of blood"* (verse 25) put her faith into action and received her healing.

In the Scriptures, the list of people who actively engaged their faith is enormous. What we can learn from these faith-filled believers is that you have to work your faith by putting action to the words you speak. You want to be healed. That is fine, but now you must do something to activate your healing. Do something that you have never done before, and take a step of faith. This will produce results beyond your wildest imagination.

> **You have to work your faith by putting action to the words you speak.**

Works of action toward the desired goal must accompany faith. Of course, you are not helping God by doing this, but you are helping yourself. Faith without works will never save anybody. It will never see anyone healed. But our works do show the sincerity of what we profess with our mouths. Faith is an action word.

> *What does it profit, my brethren, if someone says he has faith but does not have*

works? Can faith save him? If a brother or sister is naked and destitute of daily food, and one of you says to them, "Depart in peace, be warmed and filled," but you do not give them the things which are needed for the body, what does it profit? Thus also faith by itself, if it does not have works, is dead. But someone will say, "You have faith, and I have works." Show me your faith without your works, and I will show you my faith by my works. You believe that there is one God. You do well. Even the demons believe; and tremble! But do you want to know, O foolish man, that faith without works is dead? Was not Abraham our father justified by works when he offered Isaac his son on the altar? Do you see that faith was working together with his works, and by works faith was made perfect? And the Scripture was fulfilled which says, "Abraham believed God, and it was accounted to him for righteousness." And he was called the friend of God. You see then that a man is justified by works, and not by faith only. Likewise, was not Rahab the harlot also justified by works when she received the messengers and sent them out another way? For as the body without the spirit is dead, so faith without works is dead also.

(James 2:14–26)

chapter four

The Thief of Religion

*The thief does not come except to steal, and to kill,
and to destroy. I have come that they may have
life, and that they may have it
more abundantly.*
—John 10:10

One of the deadliest enemies to receiving your healing and walking in divine health is closer to you than you may actually realize. The sad part about it is that, although this enemy may be close to you in terms of its proximity, it is not easily recognized with the natural eye. This thief of health and prosperity disguises itself as a friend to you and, even worse, as a close and personal friend of God. This enemy will appear to be God's friend, perhaps even one of God's favored children. The reason for this is that this enemy understands the way God's children operate.

This enemy is also a great student—even a scholar—of human character and social development. He has degrees in religion, church history, and spiritualism. Your enemy studies and has studied church people, church actions, church nature, and church protocol for more than two thousand years. He is an expert at counterfeiting what is real. He substitutes counterfeit revivals for bona fide ones, false conversions for true ones, and simulated healings for genuine ones. He cannot originate anything. He is not an archetype. He sees something and then copies it. The problem is that he does a phenomenal job of copying. He does it so well that only the discerning eye can perceive the truth and discover the lies that this enemy so generously spreads. He is an archenemy to your healing and your overall health.

Interestingly enough, the Bible has a name for this enemy of your soul. He is called "thief." The Bible records in John 10:10 a full job description of this thief. He comes for three primary reasons—to steal, to kill, and to destroy. We know that this thief does the obvious; he steals. But he, unlike other thieves, also murders and brings destruction anywhere he is allowed.

Let's look at exactly what this thief wants to steal in the context of healing.

> *And He entered the synagogue again, and a man was there who had a withered hand. So they watched Him closely, whether He would heal him on the Sabbath, so that they might accuse Him. And He said to the man who had the withered hand, "Step forward." Then He said to them, "Is it lawful on the Sabbath to do good or to do evil, to save life or to kill?" But they kept silent. And when He had looked around at them with anger, being grieved by the hardness of their hearts, He said to the man, "Stretch out your hand." And he stretched it out, and his hand was restored as whole as the other. Then the Pharisees went out and immediately plotted with the Herodians against Him, how they might destroy Him.* (Mark 3:1–6)

In this passage of Scripture, we find Jesus bringing healing to a man with a withered hand. The Pharisees were standing close by to see if this man would receive something from Jesus, something even greater than the healing itself. Mark 3:3 lets us know that Jesus spoke two simple words: *"Step forward."* These words must have aggravated the Pharisees tremendously. But Jesus continued to speak to the man with the withered hand. Jesus told him, *"Stretch out your hand"* (verse 5). Jesus saw the man's faith in action and connected it with divine words.

The words that flow out of God's mouth are always full of burden-removing, yoke-destroying power. So this man, who had stepped forward in faith, was completely healed because of the words Jesus spoke to him.

> The words that flow out of God's mouth are always full of burden-removing, yoke-destroying power.

The Pharisees, who were in obedience to the thief, became so angry that they plotted with the Herodians to destroy Jesus. The Pharisees could not figure out a way to steal the Word from Jesus, so they became frustrated, seeking to kill and destroy the Giver of healing.

The primary thing that the thief wants to steal is the Word of God to you. If the thief can steal the Word, then he has accomplished his goal. He knows better than anyone that it is the Word that gives and sustains all life. Without the Word, every living thing would die. (See Hebrews 1:3.) Jesus told the tempter the very same thing:

> But He answered and said, "It is written, 'Man shall not live by bread alone, but by every word that proceeds from the mouth of God.'" (Matthew 4:4)

Ultimately, our very lives are contingent on the Word of God. If the thief can steal the Word, in actuality he has stolen everything.

Who Is the Thief?

We have mentioned the threefold job description of the thief. We know that he comes to steal, kill, and destroy. We know that he is an enemy of our faith and healing. But exactly who is the thief? The thief is a spirit that resides in people who have allowed tradition to become archived in their souls and spirits so strongly that nothing God is doing in the here and now can penetrate the surface. The thief is a spirit that elevates the observance of rites, rituals, and other traditions above God.

In the context of our discussion, religion is the thief that comes to kill, to steal, and to destroy. This spirit of religion was very strong in the Pharisees in biblical days. It may help to consider exactly what a Pharisee was:

> **Pharisee**: a member of a Jewish sect of the intertestamental period noted for strict observance of rites and ceremonies of the written law and for insistence on the validity of their own oral traditions concerning the law.

In the third chapter of Mark, we read that the Pharisees sought to destroy Jesus because He healed on the Sabbath. Furthermore, they sought to kill Him because He broke their religious tradition. The keepers of religious tradition will often pursue anyone who desires to break away from that tradition until he or she is destroyed.

From the definition and the biblical example, we can understand what a Pharisee was and represented. Today the Jewish sect of Pharisees is defunct. However, that does not mean that we no longer have to deal with Pharisees. The spirit that worked in them is working in modern-day types of Pharisees. A modern Pharisee is a person who honors church law, church rules and regulations, and church traditions above the law of God. A Pharisee—or one who has a religious spirit—may be a sanctimonious, self-righteous, or even hypocritical person. This religious spirit is present in churches more than ever. The thief called religious tradition, or simply religion, is worshipped above God and honored more than family relationships.

Religious tradition does not care who it hurts or offends as long as the tradition continues. In Mark 3:1–6, the Pharisees did not care if the man with the withered hand never received his healing as long as their tradition of keeping the Sabbath was upheld. This man was in desperate need of healing. Perhaps he could not work or earn a living for himself because of his physical challenge. He may even have been ostracized from the community because he was quite visibly different from everybody else. Regardless of the possible challenges that may have hindered this man from having a fruitful life, the religious leaders of the day did not care about him.

Religion denies the power and demonstration of God, and that is exactly what Pharisees do. Religion does not care who it harms as long as it remains true to its tradition. Religion and religious people are enemies to you and your healing. The religious person will make a religious excuse

for why you need to die anyway. He will make excuses for why God does not want to heal you. Religious people are enemies to the very thing that
Jesus came to give us—life and that *"more abundantly"* (John 10:10). As I have said before, religious tradition comes to steal, to kill, and to
destroy. It comes to steal the Word of God, kill its
influence on our souls and spirits, and destroy
our relationship with the King of Kings. After religion has done its job, it leaves its victims not
only dead, but also destroyed, reduced to frag-
ments, and rendered ineffective and useless.

Religion is not only a kingdom thief; it is also
a great enemy and hindrance to the Gospel of the
kingdom.

> *When anyone hears the word of the king-
> dom, and does not understand it, then the
> wicked one comes and snatches away
> what was sown in his heart.*
> (Matthew 13:19)

The wicked one referred to in this verse
snatches away, or steals, the Word that was sown
in someone's heart. Likewise, the enemy wants to
rob us of physical and spiritual health. John's
prayer for Gaius speaks to us today.

> *Beloved, I pray that you may prosper in all
> things and be in health, just as your soul
> prospers.* (3 John 2)

The Bible also declares,

> *If you diligently heed the voice of the LORD
> your God and do what is right in His sight,
> give ear to His commandments and keep*

all His statutes, I will put none of the dis-
eases on you which I have brought on the
Egyptians. For I am the LORD who heals
you.   (Exodus 15:26)

After we have received such a powerful word
from God on healing, the religious person comes
to steal that Word from us. He will insert a religious sounding word from his flesh, and often from
the devil, to counterattack the Word received from
God.

Misconceptions, the Thief's Favorite Weapon

One of the many methods that the thief em-
ploys to disrupt our connection with God long
enough for him to steal our healing is through
misconceptions. These misconceptions appear to
be true, but they are subtle and serpentine. They
are wrapped in religious phrases and words that
we have come to accept as God's Word. It is the
thief, the religious spirit, who safely delivers these
false concepts. Often they are associated with a
misinterpreted Scripture so as to give them cre-
dence and validity. Let us examine a few of these
false concepts.

> ### False Concept #1
>
> **The reason why this sickness has
> come upon you is that God is trying
> to work something good in your life.**

This lie is one of the most believed false concepts today. Sadly, many Christians accept this
as truth without questioning its validity. Satan,
who is a deceiver, has done well to fool the minds

of believers everywhere concerning the relationship between sickness and God's goodness. Oral
Roberts coined a saying that goes, "God is a good
God, and the devil is a bad devil. There is no
goodness in the devil and no badness in God." He
would often sing a song entitled, "Something
Good Is Going to Happen to You." This revelation
seems so simple, but it is very profound.

If we could only receive the truth of this
statement, our walk with Jesus would truly be
sweeter as the days go by. We often fail to recognize that there is nothing bad in God. Sickness is
bad. There is no other way to look at it. There is
no good element in sickness, nor
can anything good come from
sickness, because there is nothing in sickness that is good. One
may comment, "Well, if you get
healed, then that is good." Of
course, healing is good. However,
healing does not come from sick-
ness; healing comes from God. Thus, nothing good
can come from sickness.

> Healing does not come from sickness; healing comes from God. Thus, nothing good can come from sickness.

Many have expounded about this concept,
using this familiar verse in Romans as the scriptural basis for their "logic":

> *And we know that all things work together
> for good to those who love God, to those
> who are the called according to His pur-
> pose.* (Romans 8:28)

This has been the basis for pharisaical
statements that try to prove that your present
sickness exists because God is trying to work out
something good for you. What a gross misinter-
pretation of God's Word!

First of all, Romans 8:28 is not a Scripture that deals with justifying bad things. Rather, it deals directly with predestination and walking in your divine, God-given call or destiny for your life. The first requirement for all things to work together for good is that you love the Lord without reservation. If you do not love God, then all things will not work together for your good.

Second, you must be walking in His calling and purpose for your life in order for all things to work together for your good. If you are not walking in God's purpose for your life, then you will not see all things working together for your good. All things work for the good of those who love Him *and* are fulfilling their God-given destiny in their lives. Only those who are consistently doing these things reap the full blessing connected with this promise, because their obedience to God's call on their lives helps to establish His covenant in the earthly realm.

But how do we know that this Scripture deals with predestination and destiny? If we continue to read the verses that follow, they will plainly reveal the answer. .

> *For whom He foreknew, He also predestined to be conformed to the image of His Son, that He might be the firstborn among many brethren. Moreover whom He predestined, these He also called; whom He called, these He also justified; and whom He justified, these He also glorified.*
> (Romans 8:29–30)

The good that God wants to work in you is for you to be walking daily in divine health, free from sickness and disease.

The thief or the religious spirit is well versed in the Bible. This spirit knows Scriptures and remembers them well. I strongly advise this: As a believer, you need to become more knowledgeable than the thief is. The thief can never trick or plot against you with what you know, but rather by using what you do not know. This trick of the enemy will leave you without your healing, discouraged and ashamed. Paul gave us hope when he wrote,

> *Study to show thyself approved unto God, a workman that needeth not to be ashamed, rightly dividing the word of truth.* (2 Timothy 2:15 KJV)

> ### False Concept #2
>
> **God is glorified through our sickness. God receives glory by using sickness to teach us lessons.**

The word *glory* means "very great praise, honor, or distinction bestowed by common consent; renown." Using *glory* in the usual sense, this second false assumption means that our being sick and disabled somehow honors and esteems God. Sickness is claimed to add distinction to and exalt His name.

Glory also denotes being in a state of great splendor or prosperity. The very first mention of the word *glory* in the Bible is in the book of Genesis.

> *And he heard the words of Laban's sons, saying, Jacob hath taken away all that was our father's; and of that which was our father's hath he gotten all this glory.* (Genesis 31:1 KJV)

It is clear that Jacob did not receive praise or honor, but rather wealth. The word *glory* in this verse means wealth. If we use the word *glory* in this same way, the second misconception would suggest that our sickness increases God's abundance of wealth and riches.

It is quite apparent that either way you look at it, God does not need us to be sick in order for Him to receive glory. God is glorified as He stands alone. He does not need confirmation from anyone or anything to justify His own nature and status. His glory is attributed to Him because He remains in a class by Himself. There is none like Him in all the earth.

So, for God to use your sickness and disease as a way to garner honor and praise would be pitiful. This would put God in a mortal classification. God would be no greater than we are if He had to compete for glory status. Would you as a parent consider it praiseworthy and honorable for your own children to experience sickness? Of course you wouldn't. Then why should God the Father seek honor and glory through your sickness, your pain, your agony, and your suffering? The truth is that He does not.

God is prosperity. However, in one sense He prospers when we prosper. Just as we are absolutely ecstatic when our children prosper with a high-paying job, a solid marriage, a fine education, and a strong Christian testimony, so God is pleased when we prosper and remain in good health. This brings glory to God.

Now He was teaching in one of the synagogues on the Sabbath. And behold, there was a woman who had a spirit of infirmity eighteen years, and was bent over and could in no way raise herself up. But when Jesus saw her, He called her to Him and said to her, "Woman, you are loosed from your infirmity." And He laid His hands on her, and immediately she was made straight, and glorified God. (Luke 13:10–13)

Luke's record of the story of the woman who was healed by Jesus of an infirmity gives us some interesting details. We know that the woman was sick. We also know that she had been dealing with this sickness for about eighteen years. We also know that this illness was so severe that it somehow affected the alignment of her spine because she was bent over and could not straighten herself. Up until this point, the Scripture does not record her situation as one giving glory and honor to God.

Jesus called to the woman, which indicates that He got her attention. He spoke life into the woman when He declared, *"Woman, you are loosed from your infirmity."* Notice that God did not receive glory until after she was made straight or healed. Prior to her healing, this woman was in no shape to give glory to God. She could not give glory to God for something that He had not done.

God does not teach us lessons by putting sickness upon us. I have endeavored to crystallize this message in you: God cannot put sickness on you, because He does not have sickness to give. God teaches us lessons through His Word.

Therefore the law was our tutor to bring us to Christ, that we might be justified by faith. But after faith has come, we are no longer under a tutor. (Galatians 3:24–25)

God uses the law to teach us valuable lessons until faith in Christ brings us into the freedom of being mature believers.

All Scripture is given by inspiration of God, and is profitable for doctrine, for reproof, for correction, for instruction in righteousness, that the man of God may be complete, thoroughly equipped for every good work. (2 Timothy 3:16)

Obviously, sickness, in and of itself, cannot benefit us. Neither will sickness reprove or instruct us in righteousness. God's Word and His Word alone instructs us in righteousness. God teaches us through His Word. And God's Word is the only true basis for our faith. The apostle Paul said, *"So then faith comes by hearing, and hearing by the word of God"* (Romans 10:17).

The final consideration regarding this misconception is that God does not have to cause tragedy in your life in order to get your attention. The Scriptures let us know that when God wanted to get someone's attention, He simply spoke.

God is always speaking. God does not lack words to speak. The question we should ask is, Are we listening? Are we hearing the voice of the Lord? If we fail to recognize God's voice, we may fall into a trap set up by the devil. God may have been warning us or even instructing us. But we fail at times to listen. God uses His love, not tragedy, to draw men unto Him.

The LORD has appeared of old to me, saying: "Yes, I have loved you with an everlasting love; therefore with lovingkindness I have drawn you." (Jeremiah 31:3)

> ## False Concept #3
> ### We all have to die sometime, don't we?

The Bible gives us a real outlook on death and dying. One truth remains constant for every believer who is not caught up to meet God in the air—we all have to die. If we are alive when Jesus returns, we will not have to experience physical death as we now understand it to be. We will just take on a new "glorified" body. For those of us who will be caught up to meet Christ in the air, we will not experience physical death with all of its common associations (e.g., cessation of brain waves and heart function). We will simply pass from one reality of life to a greater reality of life, unhindered by the flesh or senses.

The Bible says,

> *So we are always confident, knowing that while we are at home in the body we are absent from the Lord. For we walk by faith, not by sight. We are confident, yes, well pleased rather to be absent from the body and to be present with the Lord.*
> *(2 Corinthians 5:6–8)*

The apostle Paul let us know that it is better to be absent from our physical bodies and to be with the Lord. He also said that while we are *"at home in the body,"* or have taken up residence in our flesh, we are absent from the Lord. We can see that while we are still fleshly minded, worldly and carnal, we are absent from the Lord. We can be fully alive in the flesh, yet dead to Christ and the things of the kingdom of God.

For to be carnally minded is death, but to be spiritually minded is life and peace.
(Romans 8:6)

If you are carnally minded, God already considers you dead. So the only way to be alive to Christ is to be dead to the world.

Let us look further:

Therefore we make it our aim, whether present or absent, to be well pleasing to Him. For we must all appear before the judgment seat of Christ, that each one may receive the things done in the body, according to what he has done, whether good or bad. (2 Corinthians 5:9–10)

This Scripture implies that we should aim at pleasing God whether we are dead or alive, *"present or absent."* How can a physically dead person be *"well pleasing"* to God? If you are dead, then you are dead. A physically dead man cannot have faith. Without faith and its proper exercise, it is impossible to please God. Yet, the apostle Paul said that it should be our aim to please God whether we are dead or alive.

The truth of the matter is that whether you are saved or whether you are a sinner, you are dead. So, if a born-again believer physically dies today and if an ungodly, unrighteous sinner physically dies today, they were both already dead before they died. The believer dies at the point of *accepting* the work of Jesus Christ on the cross and His resurrection. The sinner dies at the point of *rejecting* the work of Jesus Christ on the cross and His resurrection.

> The truth of the matter is that whether you are saved or whether you are a sinner, you are dead.

85

The believer dies to the influence of the world and its systems. The believer dies to the carnal mindset. The believer dies to the thought processes of worldly, religious, or unbelieving people.

Sinners, through rejecting Christ, have died to all possibility of life eternal. They have died to the reality of the life in the Spirit that believers so sweetly enjoy. They have died to the possibility of life and peace. Both sinners and believers are dead.

Everyone has a death appointment, and it is a one-time appointment. However, this appointment is not when you physically die. This appointment is at the altar. This altar is not necessarily in a church. It could be in a car, at the mall, in your bedroom, or even at work. The altar is the place of sacrifice. At the altar our lives are sacrificed to God as we die the final death.

Believers, after this death we will never ever die again. From the moment that we were born again, we died our final death and were relocated to a state of eternity. For Christians, eternity begins at the moment of spiritual conception, when we are born again. That moment of conception marks two significant yet seemingly antithetical events—death and life.

> For Christians, eternity begins at the moment of spiritual conception, when we are born again.

For unbelievers that truth is the same. At the point of rejecting Christ, they have birthed death to anything that is Christlike. They have birthed life to the things and sensations of the flesh that are only temporal. They have also birthed eternity to spiritual death, which is the peak of all deaths, for spiritual death is the absence of the presence of God.

God's Word declares,

> *It is appointed for men to die once, but af-*
> *ter this the judgment, so Christ was of-*
> *fered once to bear the sins of many. To*
> *those who eagerly wait for Him He will*
> *appear a second time, apart from sin, for*
> *salvation.* (Hebrews 9:27–28)

This Scripture is one that many "thieves" quote with great pride to defend their position of the inevitable reality of impending death. This Scripture is true. However, one must look at the Scripture for what it says and not what we would like it to say to accommodate entrenched theological doctrine.

As the Scripture states, men will die once. After they die, they will face judgment. Without getting too abstract, let us for one moment suspend our usual thinking about this verse. We ordinarily look at this Scripture as meaning we will all physically die one day, and after we die, we will experience Judgment Day.

That may be the commonly held meaning, but let us look at this verse in light of what we have been discussing. *"It is appointed for men to die once, but after this the judgment."* After what? After you die. After physical death? If this verse meant only physical death and then Judgment Day, this would exempt us from the coming judgment of our Lord because we are not dead in the physical sense. Yet we know from 2 Corinthians 5:10 that none of us will escape appearing before Christ's judgment seat. So, in keeping with the idea that every one of us has already died, either to the world or to life in God, this Scripture can also mean that judgment is occurring now.

So then, we are all presently being judged, not in the sense of final sentencing, but in the sense of ongoing evaluation for every work that we do, for our good and evil deeds. That judging process has begun and is going on now.

Are you fulfilling your God-given destiny? Are you right now in the purpose and plan of God for your life? If you are not, then it is not your time to die physically. As a believer, your time to die physically is when you have given everything that you are to humanity. It is your time to die when you have fulfilled your God-inspired dreams and destiny. You should not die until this has been fulfilled.

> As a believer, your time to die physically is when you have given everything that you are to humanity.

That statement strips the power from the carnal thought that substantiates premature death. If people die before age seventy, in my opinion they have died prematurely. The only exception to that rule is if the person has been martyred for a cause as Jesus, Stephen, and Dr. Martin Luther King, Jr., were. Under the old covenant, the children of Israel were promised a minimum of seventy years. If a person died prior to that age, that person was often robbed of the godly privilege of fulfilling his or her life's destiny.

> *The days of our lives are seventy years; and if by reason of strength they are eighty years.* (Psalm 90:10)

The Bible also states,

> *And the LORD God commanded the man, saying, "Of every tree of the garden you may freely eat; but of the tree of the*

*knowledge of good and evil you shall not
eat, for in the day that you eat of it you
shall surely die."* (Genesis 2:16–17)

Adam lived for a total of 930 years, yet God
said that he died when he ate the forbidden fruit.
Of course, that could not have meant physical
death, but rather spiritual death. From the moment that Adam died, God pronounced judgment
on him. He did not have a funeral service, a
preacher to deliver the eulogy, or any of the trap-
pings connected to a burial of his day.

Adam ate of the fruit, yet he lived physically
for 930 years. Methuselah, who is not known to
have done anything of lasting significance other
than having children, lived for 969 years, nearly a
millennium. Noah, who built an ark at the command of the Lord and also built the first recorded
altar, lived 950 years. Noah's son Shem lived 600
years. Eber, who was a descendant of Shem, and
who was also the head of a family in Gad, lived
464 years. These men all lived in a time when the
grace of our Lord and Savior Jesus Christ had not
been introduced, yet they all lived hundreds of
years.

Since the patriarchal period in the earthly
realm, there has been a rise of sin and lawless-
ness, environmental changes, and vast dietary
and health modifications. Today there are different cultural and customary practices than at that
time. In addition, thought processes that depend
on the natural and not the supernatural are more
prevalent now than ever. Because of these reasons, and as the result of sin's ever-magnified de-
caying effects genetically, individuals live far less
time than they would have during the days of the

Patriarchs. Today we do not see anyone living to be hundreds of years old. We must recognize that, with the advancement of technology and travel, our God-given purpose can be fulfilled in a much shorter span of time than was needed for many of the patriarchal fathers.

In our modern-day society, the average life span is about seventy-five years. With this in mind, consider the condition of the average person at death. Many have not enjoyed any of life's pleasures. Few retire with enough money for the funeral arrangements, let alone leaving an inheritance for their children. Although "ripe in age," as some often say, the average person has not even started pursuing his or her destiny. Most people have lived life paying bills and maintaining the status quo. This is not the will of God for your life. In fact, it is just the opposite.

God wants you to die empty, leaving nothing in the contents of the bodily frame that He lent to you for a season. *"It is appointed unto man once to die"* (Hebrews 9:27 KJV). Believers have already died. With that death we have inherited the benefits of the new covenant. After receiving such benefits, we are held accountable for what we do with them.

> God wants you to die empty, leaving nothing in the contents of the bodily frame that He lent to you for a season.

This is the point where judgment begins. Will you fulfill the call of God on your life? Will you allow sickness, disease, or the thief to rob you of your birthright? Or will you live out all of the days of your life and be satisfied? I pray that you will choose life.

With long life I will satisfy him, and show him My salvation. (Psalm 91:16)

*I have set before you life and death,
blessing and cursing; therefore choose life,
that both you and your descendants may
live.* (Deuteronomy 30:19)

False Concept #4

**God wants me to suffer. After all,
Jesus said that everyone should deny
himself and carry his cross.**

---

*Then Jesus said to His disciples, "If any-
one desires to come after Me, let him deny
himself, and take up his cross, and follow
Me."* (Matthew 16:24)

This has been a favorite verse used to justify
a gospel of suffering. Suffering for the Lord Jesus
Christ carries with it the highest honor. Believers
everywhere should embrace the opportunity to
suffer for the cause of Christ and His kingdom.
There is, however, a distinct difference between
suffering for Christ, self-imposed suffering, and
suffering because of sickness. Suffering for Christ
deals with a commitment that one has made to
live out the message of the Gospel of the kingdom
no matter what it takes. For making this commitment, a believer will suffer much persecution.
However, the persecution endured for the sake of
righteousness (Matthew 5:10) is a trifling matter
when compared to the blessing that one receives
through obedience and service.

Self-imposed suffering deals with the idea of
creating an atmosphere of suffering to try to earn
kingdom credit. This type of suffering is pointless
and does not bear fruit. One cannot earn righteousness or godly rewards through suffering for

an inferior cause. As with self-imposed suffering, suffering because of sickness merits neither rewards nor kingdom benefits. Since sickness is an issue that has already been dealt with and suffered for by our Lord on the cross, we no longer have to fight to obtain the promise of divine health. We simply walk in the knowledge of His truth concerning healing.

The healing plan has already been negotiated and activated by our Lord. We just need to receive the benefits. It is similar to an insurance policy. Once the policy premium has been paid, the policyholder has access to the full benefits of the policy. Many benefits may be unknown to the policyholder, yet they are still available. As soon as the policyholder becomes fully aware of the benefits package, he does not have to register again because the policy has been paid in full. Likewise, Jesus has paid our policy in full. Ever since He made the final installment on Calvary's cross, the believer has received whatever is needed. Suffering, in the sense that we have dealt with it, then becomes a choice. One may choose to suffer or one may choose to reign with Christ now and forever.

The whole concept of bearing the cross for Christ centers on our willingness to identify with Christ in ways that would normally be unconventional. We willfully take up the cross to exemplify to a dying world the hope in the Resurrection and faith in our Lord. We take up the cross in expectation that through the cross we may discover its power and the Source of its power, the Lord Jesus Christ. The cross of Christ will never be forced on an individual. It must be a choice for a worthy cause. Believers under the banner of the grace of our Lord Jesus are never called to suffer sickness, nor are we forced to bear sickness as our cross. Bearing sickness is a choice as much as bearing the cross of Christ. Sickness will lead us only to death. The cross will bring us to Christ, who will lead us to life.

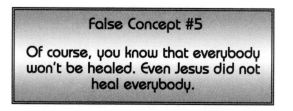

False Concept #5

Of course, you know that everybody won't be healed. Even Jesus did not heal everybody.

It is true that not all will be healed. It is true that many will die before their destiny is fulfilled. It is also true that many believers will suffer terminal sicknesses and die. Despite the reality of all those statements, it is still God's will to heal. Many argue that because all are not healed, it must be God's intention for some to remain sick.

> *The Lord is not slack concerning His promise, as some count slackness, but is longsuffering toward us, not willing that any should perish but that all should come to repentance.* (2 Peter 3:9)

From this verse we realize that God's will is that not one person in this world should perish, but rather have everlasting life. You know as well as I do that everybody will not go to heaven.

Although millions will perish in a Christless hell, it is still God's will that they inherit eternal life. Likewise, many live without receiving healing. Nonetheless, God makes it plain that He still desires for us to receive healing. God will not force salvation on anyone. In the same way He will not force anyone to receive healing. Millions of people perish because they lack knowledge of Christ. Millions are sickened to death because they lack knowledge concerning health and divine healing. People perish every day for lack of knowledge. The rate at which we perish is in direct proportion to our lack of knowledge.

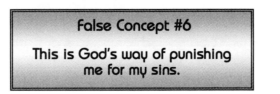

False Concept #6

This is God's way of punishing me for my sins.

Under the old covenant, God punished many for the sin of disobedience. Under the new covenant, Jesus has become our Atonement for sin. To believe that God punishes sin with sickness implies that when the sickness has either run its course or when it ends in death, you will have satisfied the obligation and made yourself righteous again before the Father. You cannot pay for your sins in that sense. Our flesh and blood would be an unacceptable payment for sin or sickness. Payment for sin requires much purer blood and far more precious flesh than our own.

If we could satisfy God through bearing our sickness as punishment for sin, then two things would be true. First, God would be a vindictive God, seeking revenge for the sins of His children. Second, Jesus' suffering, His death on the cross, and His resurrection would have been unnecessary. Neither one of these is true. Although sin is reprehensible in the eyes of God, He never sees it in the believer. Both sin and sickness have been covered and totally immersed in the blood of Jesus.

> ## False Concept #7
>
> Paul had a thorn in flesh. His thorn never left him, and I am no better than the apostle Paul.

It is true that Paul dealt with a thorn in his flesh. It is also true that the thorn never left him. However, there is not any scriptural evidence of this thorn being a sickness.

> *And lest I should be exalted above measure by the abundance of the revelations, a thorn in the flesh was given to me, a messenger of Satan to buffet me, lest I be exalted above measure. Concerning this thing I pleaded with the Lord three times that it might depart from me. And He said to me, "My grace is sufficient for you, for My strength is made perfect in weakness." Therefore most gladly I will rather boast in my infirmities, that the power of Christ may rest upon me. Therefore I take pleasure in infirmities, in reproaches, in needs, in persecutions, in distresses, for Christ's sake. For when I am weak, then I am strong.* (2 Corinthians 12:7–10)

The Scripture describes Paul's thorn in the flesh as *"a messenger of Satan,"* sent to torment him. The Greek word *aggelos*, translated here as *messenger*, is used 188 times in the New Testament. It is defined as an *angel* more than ninety-six percent of the time. It also implies a *minister* in the sense of a pastor. A derivation of the word refers to an *ambassador* of the Gospel, a commissioner of Christ, with the authority and miraculous ministry of an *apostle*. Never is it translated as being sickness or disease. The apostle Paul himself never refers to his thorn as a sickness either. The text does suggest that this thorn was a weakness to the apostle Paul. It became so bothersome that Paul pleaded with God to take it away.

Although no one knows for sure exactly what Paul's thorn was, we can theorize about a few possible ideas concerning it. We do know that it was not sickness. We do know that it was referred to as a messenger or one who carries a message. We also know that this messenger was a type of angel or person. We know as well that the message carried by the messenger was an evil or contentious message because it was delivered from Satan. The thinking individual can readily deduce that this thorn in Paul's flesh was a person who constantly came against Paul's earthly ministry in one form or another. It seems that when Paul was making progress in his apostolic mission, this messenger would come against him so vigorously that it would cause weakness to occur. Once weakness occurred, Paul's spirit was open for satanic attack, leaving him fair prey for the enemy.

This attack could have caused Paul to regress, having to make up for the time and energy spent dealing with this thorn. This may have caused Paul to look with greater intensity to the Lord for strength. This may have also been the reason why Paul said, *"I affirm,...I die daily"* (1 Corinthians 15:31). Crucifying the flesh was a daily practice in Paul's life. The development of this daily habit may be directly linked to the never-ending struggle that Paul had with this thorn in his flesh.

We do not know for certain why God did not take away Paul's thorn. We do know from life experience that external pressure can be a great character builder—if we withstand it and learn the lessons of value from it.

> We do know from life experience that external pressure can be a great character builder—if we withstand it and learn the lessons of value from it.

Paul was an avid reader, a scholar, and also was greatly used of God, having written two-thirds of the New Testament. As a Jewish boy he memorized Scripture and studied Jewish history. He later studied under the tutelage of the great philosopher Gamaliel. He was given to the body of Christ as an apostle, a missionary and church builder. Having garnered so many accomplishments, Paul might have had the propensity to believe that all of these accomplishments were attained because of his excellence and skill. This thorn may have stayed with Paul by God's permission to serve as a constant reminder of His sovereignty and power. Paul could not have fulfilled his immense divine destiny had he not been in optimal physical health and had he not had the prevailing presence of God operating in his life.

The thief, as we have mentioned repeatedly, often disguises himself in the form of religious tradition. These religious traditions can greatly obscure the vision of Christ in us, blinding us to the potential power waiting to be tapped into. Religion does not care whether or not you receive your healing. Religion does not care whether you and all of your loved ones die prematurely. Religion will be so bold as to misuse Bible Scriptures to support its stand. Beware of this deception.

Also realize that it does not take a great amount of religion to contaminate even the purest believer. Just a minute portion of religion will cause the entire healing process to malfunction. Avoid the leaven of religion, and seek a relationship with Christ the Healer.

> *Your glorying is not good. Do you not know that a little leaven leavens the whole lump?* (1 Corinthians 5:6)

chapter five

Words Count

Words are amazing. With words we express who we are, what we feel, and where we expect to go. With our words we can convey strong emotions, such as love and hate, sorrow and joy. With words we communicate our thoughts, intentions, and motives. Words are the basis for intelligent reasoning in any civilized society. Words are so powerful that they have been used to create peace as well as start world wars. Words can be more powerful than most people realize.

In this chapter we will look at the value of words and positive confessions in relationship to healing. Throughout the ages the use of words has had an incredible impact on the overall quality of life. It is also speculated that our income can increase considerably with just the knowledge and use of a few new words.

In this past century, religious people, the devil, and his staff have devalued the power of words. The enemy realizes more than believers do how powerful our words actually are. His primary mission is to keep our faith in a dormant state. He knows that if we never put words to our faith, then our faith will lack the very power needed to produce manifested results. While words may seem as insignificant and meaningless to many, they have in them the ability to create a world of peace and prosperity. While this scheme of the enemy has been productive in times past, we need to endeavor to make up for lost time by implementing words into our daily routine that will bring forth the power of God that is within.

Words Are a Creative Force

On the subject of the creative power of words, we can look to no better example than that of God Himself. One of the many names of God is Yahweh-Yatsar, who is the Lord our Creator. God is the Creator of the heavens and earth.

> *This is the history of the heavens and the earth when they were created, in the day that the LORD God made the earth and the heavens.* (Genesis 2:4)

Many recognize God as the Creator of everything that we can see in nature. How exactly did God form the heavens and the earth? Let us look at the creation story in Genesis.

> *In the beginning God created the heavens and the earth. The earth was without form, and void; and darkness was on the face of the deep. And the Spirit of God was hovering over the face of the waters.*
> (Genesis 1:1–2)

In the beginning when God created the heavens and the earth, there was absolutely nothing there. The entire earth was void, which signifies emptiness.

In Genesis 1:3, we read that God spoke, and what He spoke, He saw. But He did not see it until He spoke it. And what God spoke was based on what is inside Him. *"Then God said, 'Let there be light'; and there was light"* (Genesis 1:3). The very first thing that God gives the earth is the very thing that the earth has been rejecting since creation—light, which can be equated to knowledge. People are destroyed for lacking and rejecting the light of the knowledge of the Lord.

> *For it is the God who commanded light to shine out of darkness, who has shone in our hearts to give the light of the knowledge of the glory of God in the face of Jesus Christ.* (2 Corinthians 4:6)

God created light with His words. Light can be defined as the absence of darkness. Darkness can be defined as ignorance or a lack of knowledge. Light then can be defined as the illuminating presence of God that ushers in the spirit of knowledge and dispels the spirit of ignorance. This light is personified in the person of Jesus Christ. Wherever Christ is, there is an overwhelming presence of knowledge and an absence of ignorance.

Nevertheless, God created light with His words. God continued to use this pattern of speaking words and seeing what was spoken to create the entire creation. In the first chapter of Genesis, eight verses begin with the same words: *"Then God said"* (verses 3, 6, 9, 11, 14, 20, 24, and 26). Today we would consider such a repetitive approach to writing wordy and excessively redundant. However, God did not seem to think that His repetitious use of *"Then God said"* was at all superfluous.

God could have spoken once and then sys-tematically categorized His list of desires. Instead, He chose to repeat the action: *"Then God said... Then God said...Then God said."* Yahweh-Yatsar, the God of Creation, wanted to show through the process of creation exactly how everything would be created then and forevermore.

In fact, from the outset of the Book of Begin-nings, God was trying to set forth a precedent, a standard for ages to come: If you can conceive it and believe it in your heart and say it with your mouth, then you can have it.

Before you get upset and start thinking that this is New Age mind science, remember that the thief has stolen, counterfeited, and twisted God's principles to fit his own agenda. Nevertheless, this creative principle is true. It originated with God, who instilled it in us. God desires that we use it for the glory of His kingdom, but He gave this 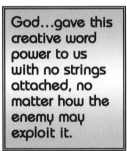 creative word power to us with no strings attached, no matter how the enemy may exploit it.

The creative power of connecting our heart beliefs and our spoken words is biblical. Nowhere in Scripture is this principle more clearly illus-trated than when the apostle Paul wrote to the Romans about salvation:

> *If you confess with your mouth the Lord Jesus and believe in your heart that God has raised Him from the dead, you will be saved. For with the heart one believes unto righteousness, and with the mouth confession is made unto salvation.*
>
> (Romans 10:9–10)

The Creative Birth Process

Using creative word power is analogous to the natural birth process. All creation begins with conception in your spirit, followed by verbal development. Once you speak creative words, you need to get in the birth position because the baby is ready to be birthed. Do not pay attention to the labor pains; the baby will come as long as you keep pushing. Keep speaking. Keep expecting that what you speak forth will be what you see.

Just as there are opposing forces during the delivery to prevent the child from being born, there will be forces against your healing that will seem to be very painful. There are times when you may feel like quitting. Just when you are about to quit, your breakthrough is one second away. Keep speaking and keep creating.

You may believe that such a creative power is reserved for God Himself. This notion could not be further from the truth. You have the same ability to create reality as God has. You are not a by-product of God, but rather a reflection of Him.

> *Then God said, "Let Us make man in Our image, according to Our likeness; let them have dominion over the fish of the sea, over the birds of the air, and over the cattle, over all the earth and over every creeping thing that creeps on the earth." So God created man in His own image; in the image of God He created him; male and female He created them.* (Genesis 1:26–27)

God created us in His image. He also gave us dominion, or ruling power. What God does in the universe, you can do in the earthly realm. If God can create an entire universe with His Word, then you can re-create your personal universe. Your world of healing and wholeness is as close as the tip of your tongue. Just speak it now! "I am healthy and whole and restored to perfect functioning by God's grace."

What Are You Creating?

You have been creating from the time you were created. At this very moment, you are the sum total of everything that you have been speaking through the course of your life. You have helped to create the world that you now enjoy or find miserable. As long as you have been able to speak words, you have been creating an atmosphere that coincides with your words. From the day you were born, your sounds created a response from your mother or whoever cared for you as an infant. When a baby cries, instinctively a mother runs to fulfill the baby's need. As the baby matures, he or she becomes more and more capable of producing sounds that are close to words, like *ba-ba*, which may mean bottle, or *ma-ma*, which usually means mother. Whatever sound a baby makes, its mother usually intuitively knows the proper response to satisfy the baby. By toddler age, children speak words of faith and power. There is virtually nothing that little children feel they cannot conquer.

> Every word that comes out of your mouth creates a manifestation of what is being spoken.

As you speak, you are creating something. Every word that comes out of your mouth creates a manifestation of what is being spoken. If you confess that you have a headache, I can guarantee that you will experience pain before long. A common confession of many adults is, "I'm broke." If you say this, do you really wonder why you don't have enough money? You have confessed your reality. Some folks have said for years, "I'll never have anything." As retirement approaches, they begin to realize that they will not have anything to sustain them financially after they retire, forcing them to work part-time at the local grocery store to make ends meet. Have you ever confessed that no one likes you? If you have, I am sure that you are experiencing the unhealthy feelings of loneliness. Your present condition can be directly linked to your heartfelt confessions of the past.

> **Your present condition can be directly linked to your heartfelt confessions of the past.**

We live in a society that takes for granted the power and unusual creative force in our words. Statements such as, "I thought I was going to die," "I died laughing," "You make me sick," "When he finds out, he's going to kill me," "He's a real pain in the neck," and many others have ushered in a spirit of sickness and death. It is just a matter of time before we will be rewarded with the fruit from sowing negative seeds with our words.

We need to have a vocabulary overhaul, a total change of what we say and how we say it. Word consciousness will help to create surroundings of abundance that God so desires us to live in. What are you creating with your words?

Children—Our Example

> *But Jesus said, "Let the little children come to Me, and do not forbid them; for of such is the kingdom of heaven."*
> (Matthew 19:14)

Children represent an element of kingdom living that adults need to mirror in order to enter into the reality of Christ's kingdom. Jesus lets us know that no one can enter the kingdom of heaven unless he becomes childlike. There is a distinct difference in being childlike and being childish. For an adult to behave in a childish manner would be for that adult to behave like a fool. Childishness denotes gross immaturity and lack of self-discipline. Childish adults are an irritation to mature adults. Seriousness is a taboo attitude for the childish adult. Everything in life is diminished to a joke.

This childish characteristic is not what Jesus desires for us to have. Instead, He invites us to be like a child or have the character and qualities of a child's spirit.

> At that time the disciples came to Jesus, saying, "Who then is greatest in the kingdom of heaven?" Then Jesus called a little child to Him, set him in the midst of them, and said, "Assuredly, I say to you, unless you are converted and become as little children, you will by no means enter the kingdom of heaven. Therefore whoever humbles himself as this little child is the greatest in the kingdom of heaven."
> (Matthew 18:1–4)

Readiness to Forgive

We must follow the many examples that children provide for us in their character qualities. One trait that is obvious in children is that they have a spirit of forgiveness. They refuse to be offended.

106

My seven-year-old daughter Eryn was playing outside with another child in our neighborhood, and this child began calling her unkind names. Eryn ran into the house, very concerned. She said, "Daddy, Jessie is calling names." It was obvious that she did not approve of his behavior. I told her that the names that she was being called should be ignored because they were not true. I also told her that her playmate only called her those names because he didn't know who she really is. "Perhaps if he knew who God made you to be, he would talk to you with a greater level of respect," I responded. Within five minutes she was playing with her friend once again. She did not take offense at his offensive remarks. She forgave him in her heart and kept moving forward. This is one of the main characteristics that Jesus demands believers to have that children possess.

As adults, we must forgive and release anything that is not Christlike out of our spirits. Adults often have a difficult time releasing the past and forgiving one another. We often retain the negative vibrations of our history so long that they become archived in our souls. This harboring of negative feelings directly connects us to the backlash of unwanted results from carrying those feelings. Children, however, have the capacity to release negative things and just forgive.

Humility

This principle of releasing requires a great amount of humility in order to initiate it. The characteristic of humility is one that we are commanded to have. If we do not walk in humility, we will never enter the kingdom of God.

Humility deals with the willingness to lessen one's importance for the greater attainment. Pride is the direct opposite of humility and is the greatest enemy to the King and His kingdom. Pride will keep anyone in a state of continual defeat. Pride will keep a person in a position of lack, poverty, and illness forever. Because pride believes it is better than everyone else is, it will never listen to the voice of the angel on assignment concerning health and well-being. In their innocence children remain open to all possibilities, which makes them candidates for divine interventions daily.

These character traits of forgiveness, releasing offense, and humility make children prized possessions in the eyes of God. The more we become like children in these characteristics, the more we become like Christ.

The Language of Children

There is yet another trait of children that is as equally rewarding as the others that were mentioned. This attribute deals with the use of words. Children seem to have no limitations when asking and believing for anything. My children believe that I have enough money to purchase the entire city of Manhattan. I probably could not convince them otherwise. In their innocence and blind faith toward the possibility of attainment, they see no limitations. And they are constantly speaking words to create their world and immediate surroundings. They constantly speak forth new clothes, the latest toys and video games, and the latest trends in child entertainment. Most children have a financial net worth of about zero. This low financial rating does not discourage them in the least. They continue to make faith demands with great confidence, and they receive the rewards of their faith over and over again. This is a reality for most children until they reach a point where life has given them reasons to no longer believe. This element of speaking words of faith is another factor that makes children God's best friends. By operating in faith, they please God.

Persistence

Another childlike characteristic that we need to develop in order to bring substance to our vision for divine health is persistence. Persistence is repeatedly, constantly, and insistently enduring with boldness, regardless of the present circumstances. Persistence is asking the same question over and over although you have already been told no several times. Persistence is the art of not quitting and never giving up.

> Persistence is repeatedly, constantly, and insistently enduring with boldness, regardless of the present circumstances.

No one has this dauntless quality as much as children do. A child does not even recognize the words "No, you cannot have it," or even "Not now." Have you ever observed a child in a toy store? The child is constantly asking for a particular toy. His mom or dad continually says, "No, not now." To my amazement, the parents almost always exit the store with a smiling child and the toy of his desire tucked tightly under his arm. Persistence pays off.

How many times will you confess your healing before you give up? You may ask me, "How many times should I confess the word of healing over my life?" My answer will always be the same. Speak the word at least one more time. Your persistence is a creative force that will yield the expected results if you don't give up.

> And let us not grow weary while doing good, for in due season we shall reap if we do not lose heart. (Galatians 6:9)

Words Heal

> He sent His word and healed them, and delivered them from their destructions.
> (Psalm 107:20)

We have already dealt with just how potent words are. We know that words can create and re-create atmospheres of greatness. Your words have the ability to bring healing to your soul. A fine example of the power of words is in the story of the centurion's servant who was healed.

> Now when Jesus had entered Capernaum, a centurion came to Him, pleading with Him, saying, "Lord, my servant is lying at home paralyzed, dreadfully tormented." And Jesus said to him, "I will come and heal him." The centurion answered and said, "Lord, I am not worthy that You should come under my roof. But only speak a word, and my servant will be healed. For I also am a man under authority, having soldiers under me. And I say to this one, 'Go,' and he goes; and to another, 'Come,' and he comes; and to my servant, 'Do this,' and he does it." When Jesus heard it, He marveled, and said to

110

those who followed, "Assuredly, I say to you, I have not found such great faith, not even in Israel! And I say to you that many will come from east and west, and sit down with Abraham, Isaac, and Jacob in the kingdom of heaven. But the sons of the kingdom will be cast out into outer darkness. There will be weeping and gnashing of teeth." Then Jesus said to the centurion, "Go your way; and as you have believed, so let it be done for you." And his servant was healed that same hour.

(Matthew 8:5–13)

Jesus was amazed by the faith of this centurion soldier. In fact, Jesus commented that He had not found such great faith in the entire kingdom of Israel, which implies that He was searching for someone to act in faith but could not find anyone. This centurion soldier had faith in the words of Jesus. He knew that if Jesus would only speak the word, his servant would be healed. In this passage Jesus did not speak any specific words that directly dealt with the servant or his condition. He spoke to the centurion soldier and told him, *"Go your way; and as you have believed, so let it be done for you."*

What the soldier believed was based on what came out of his mouth concerning Jesus' ability to heal. He said, *"But only speak a word, and my servant will be healed."* His words activated the healing power of Jesus within his servant. His faith-filled words instigated healing. Jesus told the man that his servant would be healed as he believed. The power of words can reach across the Atlantic or Pacific Ocean and beyond to cause healing to occur in someone's life. This servant never went to a Jesus Christ Miracle Healing Crusade. This servant never attended an Aaron Lewis School of Healing, yet he was healed in the very place that he was. He was healed because of what someone who believed in Christ said. Words heal.

When a godly man or woman ministers God's Word—whether at a live speaking engagement, on an audio or video cassette tape, a DVD, or a compact disc—you can be healed while listening to the words that are spoken. It doesn't have to be a special word. As long as it is a godly word, the word of faith will produce the desired results.

> *He sent His word and healed them, and delivered them from their destructions.*
> (Psalm 107:20)

Every time you listen to a minister, listen with the expectation of receiving the one word that will make all the difference in the world.

Training Your Mouth

Although you should look to ministers as anointed vessels of God, your own words should have a greater impact on you than anyone else's words. What I say about your health may be very good and very godly. When you say the same thing about your own health, then that word, your word, makes the difference. Begin to use words about yourself that will create healing and wholeness in your body.

> *The heart of the wise teaches his mouth, and adds learning to his lips. Pleasant words are like a honeycomb, sweetness to the soul and health to the bones.* (Proverbs 16:23–24)

The wisdom of this Scripture is powerful. It instructs us that we need to *teach* our mouth what to say and what not to say. When we exercise this discipline, we will add learning to our lips. If we add certain words to our vocabularies, they will cause health to come into our lives. Be sure to watch your words. Words heal.

> *There is one who speaks like the piercings of a sword, but the tongue of the wise promotes health.* (Proverbs 12:18)

Life and Death Are in Your Mouth

> *Death and life are in the power of the tongue, and those who love it will eat its fruit.* (Proverbs 18:21)

Perhaps you were raised in a culture that never gave much thought as to what people should or should not say. Maybe your relatives never thought much about the words they spoke. Possibly every time you went to a family function, you were bombarded by relatives telling you that Uncle Joe died of cancer. They shouted, "Aunt Bessie had two strokes in the past three months. Heart problems and high blood pressure run in our family. Be careful, because you might be next. When have you been checked out..." Over and over, you listen to deadly words being spoken. You just don't realize how real their words are and how much they should be avoided at all costs.

The Bible declares that *"death and life are in the power of the tongue."* Scripture does not say exactly whose tongue can usher in this spirit of death. Death can be pronounced by anyone's tongue.

113

It is our job not to speak death words or listen to or meditate on them. For the sake of our lives and destinies, we must be committed to avoid situations, surroundings, and people who continue to speak words concerning sickness and death. They may be family members or friends. They may be sincere in their approach. However, because of ignorance, over a period of time, their words may cause your demise. You must stay away from anyone who is speaking words of death.

The same verse declares that life is in the tongue as well. You are either speaking life to your life or death to your life. Every word that comes out of your mouth qualifies as a life or death word. Always think before you speak. Qualify your words. Ask yourself the question, Is what I am saying adding years or quality to my life? If the answer is no, then zip your lip.

> *He who guards his mouth preserves his life, but he who opens wide his lips shall have destruction.* (Proverbs 13:3)

The following is a list of words that you should avoid and words that will serve as their replacements. For example, instead of saying this negative, say this positive. This list is a guide as to what words create an atmosphere of life as differentiated from those that do not. Be careful to study this abridged list of power words. Begin to retrain your thinking concerning words: I can say these words, but I cannot say those words. When the discipline of watching your words becomes a daily routine, it will then become a habit. After it becomes a habit, it will become your character.

Words That Create Life List

Avoid These Statements	Instead, Say These
I am sick.	I am going through a healing process.
I can't.	With God, I can.
I hate...	I prefer...
I am afraid.	God is with me.
I am exhausted.	I will rest and recharge.
I can't take it anymore.	I'll give it another chance.
I am broke.	My money is en route to me.
I feel like I'm going to die.	I know I'm going to recover.
I am not feeling well.	I will feel better.
I never get any of the breaks.	God is my source of supply.
I've got to die sometime.	I choose life.

chapter six

The Healing–Anointing Connection

A strong connection exists between healing and the anointing. This connection is one that needs to be understood in order to walk in the divine health that God desires for us. For the most part, the anointing is one of the most misunderstood themes in Scriptures. The anointing is misunderstood mainly because it has been grossly mistaught in our churches for more than a century. Many people falsely relegate the anointing to an experience, a shake, or a quiver. Some believe that the anointing is when someone breaks out in a holy dance, or when someone speaks in tongues. Others confess that the anointing is the feeling that one gets when a favorite gospel selection is sung during Sunday morning worship. While all of these manifestations and emotions are fine when considered in the proper perspective, they are not the anointing in and of themselves.

Pentecostal Foundations

I have experienced the great blessing of having my roots in a Pentecostal background, where my beliefs were forged in the fervency of that fiery furnace. This foundation is one from which many Christians would have greatly benefited. In building a home, regardless of how solid the foundation is, the walls of the house must be erected, and the installation of the roof must be completed before the exterior of the house is considered finished. Beyond that are a myriad of things that must be installed, erected, and fabricated on the interior of the house before a certificate of occupancy can be issued.

With respect to the foundational doctrines of Christianity, no matter what the particular persuasion, the walls and roof must be installed before the exterior is completed. Unfortunately for many people, only the bare foundation has been laid in many church organizations, even after more than one hundred years of preparation.

I recognize that the foundation of any structure must be strong in order for the building to stand. However, in the building trades, it is expected that after the necessary time of foundational preparation, walls will be erected and a roof will be put on, with the intended goal of finishing the building.

> The foundation of any structure must be strong in order for the building to stand.

Many churches boast of having laid a beautiful foundation, yet they have never gone any further to finish constructing the building that God, the Great Architect, drew the plans for. The problem that exists with such a structure is that it is naked and vulnerable to all of the outside elements. Before long the foundation becomes so chipped and worn from the weathering process that nothing is able to stand on it. It has gone far past its time of expiration.

In their statements of faith, most Pentecostal organizations have delineated a theology that supports the belief in divine healing and miracles. In these written tenets of faith, you will find not just the single sentence that affirms their healing beliefs, but also the scriptural references that strongly support their position concerning healing. Many of their doctrinal creeds have one-line statements that are worded something like, "Divine healing is provided for all in the Atonement," and then they give the following Scriptures, or at least the references:

> *Surely He has borne our griefs and carried our sorrows; yet we esteemed Him stricken, smitten by God, and afflicted. But He was wounded for our transgressions, He was bruised for our iniquities; the chastisement for our peace was upon Him, and by His stripes we are healed.* (Isaiah 53:4–5)

> *When evening had come, they brought to Him many who were demon-possessed. And He cast out the spirits with a word, and healed all who were sick, that it might be fulfilled which was spoken by Isaiah the prophet, saying: "He Himself took our infirmities and bore our sicknesses."* (Matthew 8:16–17)

> *Is anyone among you sick? Let him call for the elders of the church, and let them pray over him, anointing him with oil in the name of the Lord. And the prayer of faith will save the sick, and the Lord will raise him up. And if he has committed sins, he will be forgiven. Confess your trespasses to one another, and pray for one another, that you may be healed. The effective, fervent prayer of a righteous man avails much.* (James 5:14–16)

Although the extraordinary affirmation that divine healing is available to all through the Atonement has been archived in the official, dated documents of many church organizations, very rarely do we see a demonstration of this power in action. Too many pastors in too many of these churches have members of their congregations who die prematurely. Those who struggle to live to at least the age of seventy often die of the most painful and debilitating diseases. Cancer, heart disease, and even AIDS have become all too common in the ranks of "Full Gospel" churches. The problem of unnecessary death and disease in the church persists primarily because of the fear of addressing divine healing in a straightforward, scriptural manner.

Personally, I am fed up with seeing God's precious people die prematurely. I believe that the demonstration of the power of God in the local church represents the walls of the roof of the structure. It is wonderful to know what God is capable of doing. It is far better to experience personally what God is doing. The world and the church alike are crying out for a demonstration of the power of God. They desire to see blinded eyes open, deaf ears hearing, lame legs walking, and mute mouths talking.

> The world and the church alike are crying out for a demonstration of the power of God.

Where Are the Greater Works?

It seems that everyone has become tired of the excuses that believers continue to make for why we cannot perform healing miracles in Jesus' name. Jesus once declared,

Most assuredly, I say to you, he who believes in Me, the works that I do he will do also; and greater works than these he will do, because I go to My Father. And whatever you ask in My name, that I will do, that the Father may be glorified in the Son. (John 14:12–13)

More than two thousand years have elapsed since Jesus sacrificed His body. If not now, when will we ever accomplish the work that He commands us to do? No longer can people of faith hide behind statements of faith or declarations of belief or creeds or whatever they are termed. What we say we believe must be demonstrated by our actions, not just expressed in articulately phrased words.

> What we say we believe must be demonstrated by our actions, not just expressed in articulately phrased words.

The apostle Paul left us with a sound thought concerning our speech as it relates to the power of God.

And I, brethren, when I came to you, did not come with excellence of speech or of wisdom declaring to you the testimony of God. For I determined not to know anything among you except Jesus Christ and Him crucified. I was with you in weakness, in fear, and in much trembling. And my speech and my preaching were not with persuasive words of human wisdom, but in demonstration of the Spirit and of power, that your faith should not be in the wisdom of men but in the power of God. (1 Corinthians 2:1–5)

We are experiencing a shortage of ministers of healing in the church of the Lord Jesus Christ.

Those who have legitimately been given the gift of faith, the gifts of healings, and the power to work miracles have buried their gifts in the sand because of the wrongful actions of a few charlatans who have risen in the ranks of preachers in the past several decades. This hiding has caused several distressful conditions to occur. The most obvious one is that millions have and will continue to die prematurely because believers who have the power of Jesus to heal are not doing what God has commissioned them to do. Another difficulty is that the church of the Lord Jesus Christ has become a living joke to the world. We talk big talk about Jesus, but we don't show the world the truth of what we say.

In the final analysis, we have *"a form of godliness but* [are] *denying its power"* (2 Timothy 3:5). When we deny the power of God, we are, in effect, denying God Himself.

Sadly, the gross neglect of our God-given mandate to heal the sick has created a universe filled with sick and diseased people. This problem of illness that the church refuses to deal with because of the possibility of being falsely accused or talked about publicly has given rise to the New Age and the mind science movements. Both of these movements have no fear in preaching a message of healing, wholeness, and prosperity. They preach on the power of the mind to heal the body, yet exclude the prerequisite of having the mind of Christ to activate the process. Unfortunately, we have allowed the precious God-given gifts of healing and faith to be tampered with

> Sadly, the gross neglect of our God-given mandate to heal the sick has created a universe filled with sick and diseased people.

and usurped by anti-Christian forces. Worse still, they are more consistent than Christians in the pursuit of attaining wholeness and peace.

The Bible lets us know that healing belongs to the children of God first.

> *But Jesus said to her, "Let the children be filled first, for it is not good to take the children's bread and throw it to the little dogs."* (Mark 7:27)

The world is craving what we the believers possess, and what believers have is dangerous. We have a weapon that no other weapon can stand against. This weapon is guaranteed to kill the very root of sickness and disease on contact. The faster we recognize the power of God within us—which is the anointing—the more rapidly we will begin to advance beyond the kingdom of darkness and bring light to every creature. Humanity is waiting for the anointing.

The Anointing Defined

What exactly is the anointing? The word *anointing* is not just another commonly used word whose real meaning can easily be grasped from its definition in a good dictionary. Rather, since it is a spiritual word, it needs to be defined in spiritual terms from a scriptural perspective.

To discover this definition, let us first look at a New Testament reference:

> *God anointed Jesus of Nazareth with the Holy Spirit and with power, who went about doing good and healing all who were oppressed by the devil, for God was with Him.* (Acts 10:38)

This verse helps us to understand what the anointing is and what it does. This verse says, *"God anointed Jesus of Nazareth with the Holy Spirit and with power."* Here we find that the anointing is the power of God the Holy Spirit. God anointed Jesus with His power and His Spirit. If it is God who anointed Jesus and the anointing came from God, then it is God's power. This verse further says that this power enabled Jesus to do good things, namely heal the sick and deliver people from demonic oppression: *"Jesus...went about doing good and healing all who were oppressed by the devil."* The good that Jesus did pertained to healing. Jesus was anointed to heal.

A Scripture that further clarifies the meaning of the anointing is one that we find in Isaiah:

> *It shall come to pass in that day that his burden will be taken away from your shoulder, and his yoke from your neck, and the yoke will be destroyed because of the anointing oil.* (Isaiah 10:27)

When the oil of the anointing comes on a person, we can expect two things to occur. First, the anointing causes all burdens to be removed. Second, the anointing causes all yokes to be destroyed. These burdens and yokes include sickness, disease, debt, worry, and fear.

Thus, we can see from Scripture what the anointing is and what the anointing does. Combining the information we have gleaned from Acts 10:38 and Isaiah 10:27, we can give a complete definition for the word *anointing*:

anointing: the burden-removing, yoke-destroying power of God

The word *anoint,* as it is used in the old covenant, means to rub with or to smear on oil. Oil symbolizes the presence of the Holy Spirit covering or resting on the servant of God. Naturally, when applied on a person, oil will eventually rub off or otherwise disappear, implying the need for more oil to be smeared upon the individual in order to maintain its effectiveness. Likewise, in the Old Testament sense, the presence of the Holy Spirit had to be repeatedly sought because it did not permanently rest on a person.

Today, because the Holy Spirit indwells us believers, this anointing is resident within us. The anointing lies dormant within us, but in response to an external need, the anointing is aroused within us and rises to supply the answer to that need.

Thus, the anointing is not for the individual but for others. The anointing always carries with it a God-given assignment that must be completed by the person who is anointed. God never anoints people just so they can claim they are anointed, but rather for a specific purpose.

> The anointing always carries with it a God-given assignment that must be completed by the person who is anointed.

For example, Jesus was anointed to heal the sick and free people from demonic oppression. David and Solomon were anointed to be kings of Israel. Aaron and his sons were anointed to serve as priests. The anointing comes upon an individual to accomplish a particular assignment from the Lord. The Spirit anoints us to preach, teach, and to be witnesses.

God never wastes the gift of His anointing. The anointing never shows up to do nothing.

Every time the anointing comes, it always removes burdens and destroys yokes.

In commercialized Christianity we have made the words *anointing* and *anointed* buzz words to spruce up our advertisements and brochures. Many times I have seen flyers that declare a certain man or woman of God is anointed. "Come see the anointed man of God, Evangelist Too-Big from Los Angeles! Bring the sick, the lame, the diseased, because the anointing will be there!" You, too, may have seen or heard a similar advertisement.

Having been to such meetings myself, I always grieve for the sick people who took a chance and came, believing that they would be healed, only to have been disappointed. Had they only known how common the word *anointing* has become, they would have checked themselves before making that step and finding out that no one at the meeting was anointed, and the anointing was not even mentioned. When believers make the claim of being anointed, it must be backed with a heavenly guarantee. If we are truly operating in the power and might of the Lord, then we cannot fail. We must begin to operate in a strong anointing and expect results.

> When believers make the claim of being anointed, it must be backed with a heavenly guarantee.

If you attend a meeting, a church, or a service, and your burdens are not being lifted and your yokes are not being destroyed, then you are not in an anointed atmosphere. Christians tend to conjure up a facade of the anointing to look good to others, yet produce nothing. Simply stated, an anointed man or woman is one who produces spiritual results. If the church you attend always has members who are sick and shut in, that church is not anointed. Of course, from time to time a prayer need for an individual in the congregation does arise. However, these needs will not be commonplace in a ministry if it is an anointed ministry.

The anointing is God's ability operating through mankind. With the anointing of God, we become supernatural beings. With God's anointing we have no restraints or limitations. Sickness and disease are burdens and yokes that hinder godly progression in this life and ultimately hinder the advancement of the kingdom. Both sickness and disease are eliminated when the anointing of God shows up. Nothing unlike God can stand against the anointing and live.

The Anointed One

Finally, in regard to the anointing, let's consider the name of Christ by focusing on its meaning. *Christ,* as used in the new covenant, corresponds to *Messiah* in the old covenant. *Messiah* is the Hebrew word that means the Anointed One. *Christ* is the Greek word bearing the same intent, the Anointed One. Every time we see *Christ* in Scripture we must look at it for its real worth. The Lord Jesus Christ is the Lord Jesus, *the Anointed One.* With what is the Lord Jesus anointed? The Lord Jesus is anointed with the all-encompassing power of God.

As we look at the Christ figure, we must look at Him from many perspectives. Christ is the power and demonstration of God. Christ represents the anointing and the very substance with which He was anointed. Christ is the action word in the Godhead as it relates to humanity. It is the Spirit of Christ that convicts men to righteousness. It is the Spirit of God in Christ who raised Jesus from the dead. (See Romans 8:9–11.) The Spirit of Christ must be present in order for the believer to be caught up to meet Him in the air.

Every time Christ appears, burdens are removed, and yokes are destroyed. When the anointing comes, it is because Christ has come. Christ can never come without His anointing. Christ and His anointing are one in the same. They are inseparable.

In fact, we would cause no injury to the Holy Word to interchange the words *Christ* and the *anointing* or the *Anointed One*. For the sake of arriving at a deeper understanding, let's go through this worthwhile exercise. Here are several Scriptures in which I have substituted *the Anointed One* wherever *Christ* was originally written:

> *To them God willed to make known what are the riches of the glory of this mystery among the Gentiles: which is* [the Anointed One] *in you, the hope of glory.*
> (Colossians 1:27)

> *Then Peter said, "Silver and gold I do not have, but what I do have I give you: In the name of Jesus* [the Anointed One]*of Nazareth, rise up and walk.*   (Acts 3:6)

> *Daily in the temple, and in every house, they did not cease teaching and preaching Jesus as* [the Anointed One].   (Acts 5:42)

> *For many will come in My name, saying, "I am* [the Anointed One]*," and will deceive many.*   (Matthew 24:5)

But put on the Lord Jesus [the Anointed One], and make no provision for the flesh, to fulfill its lusts.   (Romans 13:14)

For "who has known the mind of the LORD that he may instruct Him?" But we have the mind of [the Anointed One].
                                    (1 Corinthians 2:16)

He said to them, "But who do you say that I am?" Peter answered and said, "The [Anointed One] of God."   (Luke 9:20)

Have you ever recognized that *the Anointed One,* who lives in you, is the hope of your glory? It is the mandate of every believer and minister to teach and preach *the Anointed One* everywhere we go. We need to wear *the Anointed One* as a garment to ensure that our fleshly nature will not control us. Begin now and continue using this wonderful method of perceiving Christ for who He really is. He is not a mythological figment of our imagination. Neither is Christ an unreachable, unattainable goal in the mind of wishful thinkers. He is Deity, yet we can touch Him. He is and will always be *the Anointed One.*

Pride, the Assassin of the Anointing

The fear of the LORD is to hate evil; pride and arrogance and the evil way and the perverse mouth I hate.   (Proverbs 8:13)

Pride is the mask of one's own faults.
                                    —*Jewish Proverb*

Arrogance is a disease that makes everyone sick except the one who has it.
                                    —*Bob Yandian*

The nobler the blood, the less the pride.
—*Danish Proverb*

Pride goes before destruction, and a haughty spirit before a fall. Better to be of a humble spirit with the lowly, than to divide the spoil with the proud.
(Proverbs 16:18–19)

Pride is usually evidence of a poor self-concept and low self-esteem.
—*Myles Munroe*

For from within, out of the heart of men, proceed evil thoughts, adulteries, fornications, murders, thefts, covetousness, wickedness, deceit, lewdness, an evil eye, blasphemy, pride, foolishness. All these things come from within and defile man.
—*Jesus* (Mark 7:21–23)

Pride is an admission of weakness; it secretly fears all competition and dreads all rivals.   —*Fulton John Sheen*

Idleness and pride tax with a heavier hand than kings and governments.
—*Benjamin Franklin*

He who conceals his disease cannot expect to be cured.   —*Ethiopian Proverb*

A man's pride will bring him low, but the humble in spirit will retain honor.
(Proverbs 29:23)

> **While it is impossible to kill the Anointed One, it is very possible to kill the anointing.**

There is no greater murderer to the anointing than pride. Please understand that while it is impossible to kill the Anointed One, it is very possible to kill the anointing. The anointing for healing can very easily be destroyed with the smallest amount of pride. Pride is and always has been an archenemy of the kingdom of God. Its only intention is to destroy and tear down.

Pride is a demonic spirit that Jesus dealt with repeatedly in the lives of the Pharisees. In a previous chapter, I discussed the dangers concerning the religious spirit that lives in our churches and ministries. Even more noxious is when this spirit lives in our souls. This spirit has a power pack that continually fuels it in case it needs recharging. That boost is called pride.

Pride is the very element that encouraged the Pharisees to continue their onslaught against Jesus. They wanted more than anything to stop the continuous flow of His anointing. They wanted the healings to cease. They were tired of seeing people raised from the dead. It frustrated them when *the Anointed One* set demonically oppressed people free. They wanted to stop the flow of His anointing. However, they understood that the only way to stop the flow of the anointing was to stop *the Anointed One* Himself. As long as *the Anointed One* was alive, His anointing would be working in the lives of everyone with whom He came into contact. Pride became a temporary solution to the religious spirit's permanent problem. If enough pride is present, it can clog and destroy the flow of God in the life of anyone.

Pride always seeks to discover ways to do everything better than God does. Satan himself proved this to be true by his haughty attitude toward Yahweh-Yatsar, the Lord our Creator.

"How you are fallen from heaven, O Luci-fer, son of the morning! How you are cut

> *down to the ground, you who weakened the nations! For you have said in your heart: "I will ascend into heaven, I will exalt my throne above the stars of God; I will also sit on the mount of the congregation on the farthest sides of the north; I will ascend above the heights of the clouds, I will be like the Most High."* (Isaiah 14:12–14)

Proud people cannot receive instructions from anyone they deem to be spiritually less than or beneath them. For the most part, no one ever measures up to their self-inflated standards. The prideful person is usually self-righteous, self-centered, and immeasurably egotistic. It is almost unheard of for a prideful person to admit a failure or apparent insufficiency in his character or spiritual nature.

> **Proud people cannot receive instructions from anyone they deem to be spiritually less than or beneath them.**

Prideful individuals cannot accept any revelation or insight into the Scriptures that they have not personally had before. You may hear a prideful person say, "I have read the Bible from cover to cover several times, and I have been in the church all of my life, but I have never heard any such thing." They measure what God may be doing depending on whether or not they gave God permission to be God at that particular time. They continually need to set their approval on the works of God. What they do not understand, they quickly label as not being from God.

Pride-filled people usually do not do much research because they believe they already know everything. They read only the Bible—usually limited to the King James Version—because they claim that any other Christian writings, or even other Bible versions, contaminate the purity of the Holy Scriptures. Prideful people are full of ignorance, yet they take pride in the little they do know.

If you take a quick mental census of the prideful people you know, I can guarantee you that the majority of them suffer with sickness of some sort. Because pride-filled people are spiritually sick, they are usually physically ill, too. If they have followers, most of them also experience constant

> **The suffocating presence of pride smothers the anointing and healing.**

sickness. The suffocating presence of pride smothers the anointing and healing.

A Model of Pride

Several years ago, I was invited to conduct a healing service by a pastor at a church in a neighboring city. I preached and taught that healing and miracles are as much a part of our present-day experiences as they were in the days when Jesus walked with His original disciples. The power of God was mighty in the service.

At the right moment, I began to pray for the sick. For the first time, God used me to give words of wisdom and words of knowledge to the people I was praying for. It was obvious even to the skeptical onlooker that I was operating in the anointing power of the Anointed One. People were being healed of all kinds of sicknesses and diseases. Manifestations were taking place right before our eyes. A person who had been tormented by a spirit of homosexuality was immediately set free from that insidious spirit by the Anointed One. No one questioned whether God was moving in an extraordinary manner or not. We all knew He was.

The Lord drew my attention to a woman who was in her early sixties and told me to ask her if I could pray for her. As the Lord commanded, I obeyed. To my surprise, when I approached her, she openly refused my prayer. The Lord then told me to give her this word: "I know that you have been suffering with a terminal form of cancer; however, if you allow me to lay hands on you, this night you will be healed." After I spoke those words, all of her fellow churchgoers began to cry, shout, and intercede on her behalf. Unknown to me, this lady was suffering with the identical problem that God told me to tell her. Her pastor and the members knew, but I did not. She still refused. Sensing the urgency, I pleaded with her at least three more times. She still refused. I then said to God, "Lord, I did what You asked me to do." At that moment the Lord released her from my spirit. Nearly two weeks later, the pastor buried the same woman.

When he called me to tell me about her death, he shared some information that I had not known. He told me that she was an original member of the church. In fact, she was one of the founding members. She was a very staunch Apostolic Pentecostal believer. She told him that she did not want to receive my word for various reasons. One reason was that I was too young. At the time, I was in my mid-twenties. She had been raised to believe that young men did not possess as strong an anointing as that of an elderly person. She also took offense at the strong message that I taught on healing. Although I used Scriptures to validate my position, she contended that this approach to healing was unfamiliar to her theology, so it could not be from God. Finally, she felt that I was unqualified to lay my hands on her. She believed that only the bishops of her denomination had the right to lay hands on her.

To summarize all that I have said, this lady died simply because of her pride. Although there were others at that same service who were healed of cancer, she died. The anointing to heal cancer was present and strong, yet the spirit of pride blocked its ability to heal her. Cancer was only the catalyst in her demise. The true cause of her death was an overdose of the spirit of pride.

Pride must be avoided at all costs. It is an affront to God. If pride is not destroyed, it will lead to rebellion of the worst kind. The pride-filled woman literally rebelled against the Word of God. I taught God's message of healing straight from 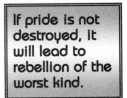 the Bible, and I told her what God told me to tell her. Although she knew that what I said was true, she still rebelled, not against me, but against God's Word. I am only a messenger of God.

As with any sin or spirit of the devil, pride cannot stay in its original form for long. It always seeks to evolve into a stronger form. As an unchecked cancer grows in the human flesh until it has taken control over the entire physical body, so it is with the sin of pride. An unwillingness to be taught by another person—no matter what age, race, or style of Christianity—will lead to the development of a religious spirit.

God cannot use someone with an unteachable spirit. The religious spirit carries with it a strong spirit of pride. Unchecked pride then becomes outright rebellion. God considers rebellion to be as diabolical as witchcraft.

> *For rebellion is as the sin of witchcraft, and stubbornness is as iniquity and idolatry. Because you have rejected the word of the LORD, He also has rejected you from being king.* (1 Samuel 15:23)

At the point of full-blown rebellion, God has two options. He will either cast the rebellion out of you, or He will cast you out of the rebellion. Either way, something has to die. God especially hates pride. When He identifies it in individuals, He cannot prosper or bless them.

> *Yes, all of you be submissive to one another, and be clothed with humility, for "God resists the proud, but gives grace to the humble."* (1 Peter 5:5)

Beware of pride! It kills the anointing!

chapter seven

Scriptural Healing Methods

With a bit of concern, I am approaching our next topic of discussion, various methods of healing. Because I reverence the sovereignty of God, I realize that any delineation of His ways of healing that I am able to present to you can only be a very abridged listing. God has millions of ways to bring healing to you. With that in mind, let's look at a few of these ways that are mentioned in Scripture.

I realize that for the believing person just one method will suffice. There is no method that is better than another. When one works, that is all that matters. Of course, the very best method is to live in a perpetual state of divine health. Divine wholeness should be the ultimate goal of every believer through the power of the Anointed One.

While the following list is brief, it may be comprehensive for you. As I mentioned, just one method will be as exhaustive a list as you need, as long as it works.

Repentance and Belief

Perhaps the most basic method of healing is true repentance and belief in the message of the Gospel. For many, this vital element is one that appears to be quite cumbersome.

Repentance must always precede faith, for repentance deals with the state of mind. True repentance deals with changing what you once thought and replacing those old thoughts with new information. The new thinking pattern then makes an immediate demand of the person to act accordingly and so causes the fruits of the change to be seen.

For example, if I were an alcoholic and I were convicted to quit that lifestyle, I would need to repent. Thus, the first thing I must do is change my mind about alcohol, its consumption, and its negative effects on my body and my whole life. Once I have changed my mind concerning those things, then and only then will my fruit remain. However, if I gave up drinking without having really changed my mind, it would not be long before I started drinking again.

A change of mind is essential to true repentance. This concept also applies to physical, spiritual, and emotional healing. Everyone has opinions concerning healing, faith healers, and divine healing in general. Millions have died in recent years because they refused to change their minds concerning what they heard from enemies of God and enemies of faith. They listened to people on radio and television condemning healing. They read books that dealt with why people should not be healed and that cautioned readers to stay away from anyone claiming to have the power or gifting to heal. This mindset of negative information has caused millions to become so rigidly closed to other possibilities that they cannot pass a very basic yet vital test.

A change of mind is essential to true repentance.

Belief in the Gospel is not attainable unless you change your mind, and changing your mind implies that you have replaced your thoughts with something of greater value. To believe that you can successfully change your mind yet not install new information is ludicrous. An empty mind is just as susceptible to human failure as a mind that is pridefully full of error. One very simple way to receive your healing is to change your old mind, block out what the critics may say, and believe and receive the fresh information of the Gospel of the kingdom.

> *Now after John was put in prison, Jesus came to Galilee, preaching the gospel of the kingdom of God, and saying, "The time is fulfilled, and the kingdom of God is at hand. Repent, and believe in the gospel."*
> (Mark 1:14–15)

The Laying On of Hands

The practice of the laying on of hands has been borrowed from Christianity by an excessive number of modern-day and ancient religions. This practice is one of great significance. It is also one of the more popular methods employed in healing circles today. It is and always will be a powerful method of transferring God's gift of healing to one who is sick. The practice of laying on of hands simply involves the courier and the receiver. The delivery person is the one who administers the gift. The receiver is the one who waits in faith-filled expectation for manifested results.

It does not matter where you touch as much as the touch itself matters. There are times when I have prayed for a person with lame legs or with a slipped disc and never touched the affected area. There are no set rules concerning the procedure, except that never should any impropriety occur or even be able to be misconstrued. Most of the time, I lay hands on the head of the person. The head of the individual represents the main supply source from which all other areas of the body feed. The head also represents the soul, will, and intellect of humankind. The reason that I do touch is to make a point of contact with the person in need. This point of contact is used as the focal point where our faith can join and be confirmed.

At the point of touching, I begin to pray for the individual in the name of the Lord Jesus Christ. I then invoke the Spirit of the Anointed One to come upon the person being prayed for. Because of God's mercy and grace, the person receives healing.

The laying on of hands is a method that Jesus Himself not only used, but also commanded us to use when praying for the sick.

> *And these signs will follow those who believe: In My name they will cast out demons; they will speak with new tongues; they will take up serpents; and if they drink anything deadly, it will by no means hurt them; they will lay hands on the sick, and they will recover.* (Mark 16:17–18)

Jesus Himself laid hands on a leper and cleansed him.

> *Now a leper came to Him, imploring Him, kneeling down to Him and saying to Him, "If you are willing, You can make me*

clean." Then Jesus, moved with compassion, stretched out His hand and touched him, and said to him, "I am willing; be cleansed."   (Mark 1:40–41)

Through Jesus' example, we see that the laying on of hands was practiced in Bible times. In fact, the laying on of hands is a biblical doctrine.

Therefore, leaving the discussion of the elementary principles of Christ, let us go on to perfection, not laying again the foundation of repentance from dead works and of faith toward God, of the doctrine of baptisms, of laying on of hands, of resurrection of the dead, and of eternal judgment.
                                   (Hebrews 6:1–2)

The doctrine of laying on of hands is one that is considered to be one of the elementary principles of Christ. When the laying on of hands is practiced in the name of the Lord Jesus, the Anointed One, healing will occur.

Anointing with Oil

Anointing with oil is another scriptural method that has been effectively used in times past and also presently. When Jesus sent out the twelve disciples to do the work of the ministry, He gave them specific instructions concerning ministry protocol. After they received His instructions, they went out preaching repentance. These are the results of their preaching:

And they cast out many demons, and anointed with oil many who were sick, and healed them.   (Mark 6:13)

The disciples used this method not only to heal the sick, but also to cast out various demons. It is evident that there is some element in the oil that rids people of demons and sickness. While we recognize that the oil alone has no healing value, we do know that the oil coupled with faith in God produces phenomenal results.

Please understand that without the element of faith operating, the oil may as well stay in the bottle. I have preached at hundreds of churches around the United States and the Caribbean. Often I have noticed a big bottle of anointing oil sitting on the podium. Although the oil is usually used regularly, people in these congregations still remain sickly. The reason they remain sick is because we have placed more value in the anointing oil than in the One who anoints the oil. When our faith lies in any substance other than the substance of Christ Himself, we become idolatrous. We are then no different from the workers of witchcraft and sorcery.

> **When our faith lies in any substance other than the substance of Christ Himself, we become idolatrous.**

While this mechanism is one of many that have yielded favorable results, we cannot put more trust in the method than in the One who empowers the method to prosper, Christ, the Anointed One.

Faith in Christ will prosper the method of anointing with oil. If we do not anoint in His name, it remains useless. Only in His name will healing be attained. Because this method is one that God's Word recommends, it is one that should be considered and practiced. When people in the local church became ill, James suggested that they seek out an elder to anoint them with oil.

Is anyone among you sick? Let him call for the elders of the church, and let them pray over him, anointing him with oil in the name of the Lord. And the prayer of faith will save the sick, and the Lord will raise him up. And if he has committed sins, he will be forgiven. (James 5:14–15)

Notice that the text specifically states that the prayer of faith is what will save the sick. The anointing oil is only a means by which God transmits the healing through the connection of prayer and faith.

Without the prayer of faith, healing will not occur, even if you are immersed in anointing oil. Pastors have been guilty of using oil as a substitute for the anointing. I have used anointing oil when I pray for the sick. Most of the time, however, I do not use anointing oil. The reason for this is that I personally believe that God will anoint me with His oil and presence. 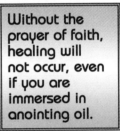 When the oil of God comes upon me, whoever I touch receives the touch of the Lord, because His presence is upon me. The anointing oil is symbolic of, but not a substitute for, the power and presence of God.

Church Elders

James wrote something of great value that needs to be mentioned before we continue. The verse states, *"Is anyone among you sick? Let him call for the elders of the church."* The responsibility lies with the sick to seek out someone in the church who will pray for them. Nowhere in the

Scriptures will you find an incident of a priest or a prophet or even Jesus searching for people who were in need of a healing touch. The afflicted, sick, tormented, or diseased individuals always sought a man. They did not seek just any man. They sought a man who carried the fragrance of the oil of God upon him. They looked for one who was anointed with oil to pray for them.

Today we find many people who become disgruntled with pastors and evangelists for not seeking them out when they are ill. Instead, they need to take personal responsibility in the situation and *"call for the elders."*

Modern-day ministers are supposed to continue what Jesus started as He ministered. We are to adopt the priorities Jesus set: *"For the Son of Man has come to seek and to save that which was lost"* (Luke 19:10). Thus, our primary calling is to seek and save those who are in ignorance of the light and wisdom of Christ, not to seek out believers who are sick to bring healing to them. If the latter became our first priority, it would only hinder the progress of spreading the kingdom message.

The sick are required to call upon the elders of the church. Elders are not limited to the clergy and boards of elders so labeled in most local assemblies. Eldership can be extended, at least unofficially, to any mature believer who has been walking with the Lord and has a firm faith and understanding of the practices and procedures of spiritual healing. In fact, this involvement of the laity helps to advance the kingdom of God. This interdependence among one another and dependence on God will help establish a priesthood of all who believe. This will encourage and strengthen pastors so that every part of the ministry does not fall upon their shoulders.

Holy Communion

> *Therefore whoever eats this bread or drinks this cup of the Lord in an unworthy manner will be guilty of the body and blood of the Lord. But let a man examine himself, and so let him eat of the bread and drink of the cup. For he who eats and drinks in an unworthy manner eats and drinks judgment to himself, not discerning the Lord's body. For this reason many are weak and sick among you, and many sleep. For if we would judge ourselves, we would not be judged. But when we are judged, we are chastened by the Lord, that we may not be condemned with the world. Therefore, my brethren, when you come together to eat, wait for one another. But if anyone is hungry, let him eat at home, lest you come together for judgment.*
> (1 Corinthians 11:27–34)

One of the less common times that people avail themselves of God's healing is when the sacrament of Holy Communion is being observed. Yet this is a prime time to take full advantage of the healing benefits made possible through our Lord's sacrifice. During this observance believers recognize the blood that was shed for us all when Jesus died. We recognize that without the shedding of blood there would not be remission for sins.

> *For this is My blood of the new covenant, which is shed for many for the remission of sins.* (Matthew 26:28)

As we have learned previously, this same blood of Jesus has sufficient power to deal with the results of original sin, known as sickness and disease, as well as sin itself. When we partake in Communion, we observe the blood for what it is. It is the sacrificial blood of Christ. We observe it for what is does. It cleanses us from all unrighteousness or anything that is not right within us. This includes all sicknesses and diseases.

We continue to observe our Lord when we partake of His body.

> *And as they were eating, Jesus took bread, blessed and broke it, and gave it to them and said, "Take eat; this is My body."* (Mark 14:22)

Partaking of the Lord's body is the point at which the healing power of Jesus either comes to you or goes away from you. The blood that Jesus shed provided the necessary payment for the insurmountable debt that was owed by humanity. However, properly partaking of the body of Christ gives us a key into the kingdom of His love.

Have you ever been locked out of your house? I have been locked out of my home before. It is not a good feeling to be outside in the cold when you know your warm bed is inside waiting for you. All of your belongings are inside the house. All of your stuff is paid for. You owe nothing on the valuables in the confines of your home. The best that life has to offer is inside your home. Yet, you cannot enter because you lost your key. Until you find your key, you will be barred from every good thing inside your home. If you decide to break into your house, the local authorities may arrest you, not realizing that the house belongs to you. This scenario is analogous to our observing the Lord's body.

When we properly observe the Lord's body, we gain entrance into the benefits that were secured for us on the cross. When we properly observe the Lord's body, we recognize the vastness and diversity within the house of the Lord. Properly discerning the Lord's body extends to combating the societal ills that have crept into the church, such as racism and racial prejudice, sexism, denominationalism, and religious intolerance.

> *For he who eats and drinks in an unworthy manner eats and drinks judgment to himself, not discerning the Lord's body. For this reason many are weak and sick among you, and many sleep.*
> (1 Corinthians 11:29–30)

The Scripture declares that the reason why people are sick and die before their time is because they refuse to discern the Lord's body. They do not grasp or, even worse, refuse to accept and recognize those who are a part of the body of Christ. This attitude of spiritual superiority will cause believers to experience continual sickness and possibly premature death.

As a child, I can remember the old saints drilling me about who was not born-again versus who was. Baptists, Methodists, Anglicans, Episcopalians, Lutherans, and Wesleyans were just not saved, or so I was taught. I was told that the reason they were not saved was simply because they were not a part of our denomination. Those people did things that we just were not permitted to do and went places that were off-limits for us.

Because of our doctrinal differences, we were taught that we were on a higher spiritual level with God.

Although thousands of people in non-Pentecostal churches were being filled with the Holy Spirit during the charismatic renewal and movement of the 1960s and 1970s, my denominational affiliation continued to discount and disregard the sovereign move of God in the lives of thousands of mainline churchgoers.

I also clearly remember that there were a large number of sick people in the organization with which I was associated. Premature death had become all too commonplace for the "real saints" and even for their children.

Since I was so young, I did not understand why the godly people I was around suffered with sicknesses for so long and so severely. As my understanding began to mature, I began to grasp the importance of recognizing the Lord's body. I have no right to determine who is or who is not a part of His body based on my limited theological interpretations and understanding of Scripture. The clear way to determine if people belong to the body of Christ is by their confession of faith and by the fruit that is produced from that confession over time.

In the event that my brothers or sisters lack knowledge on a particular subject that is valuable to their spiritual sustenance and vitality, it becomes my job to bring knowledge and light to them. If Christians don't understand the value of operating in the gifts of the Spirit (see 1 Corinthians 12), it is my job to enlighten them, not condemn them. If, after being enlightened, they still reject the truth, it is not my job to disconnect them from the entire body of Christ. It is my obligation to continue to pray for them to receive the light concerning the truth of God's Word.

Properly discerning the Lord's body is a crucial element in walking in divine health. The next time you partake in the sacrament of Holy Communion, be sure to acknowledge the blood of Jesus and its power to heal. Be sure to recognize and accept the body of the Lord Jesus. Since Christ's flesh was torn once, do not participate in any condemning activities that would create new wounds and separations in His body.

> **Since Christ's flesh was torn once, do not participate in any condemning activities that would create new wounds and separations in His body.**

Be aware that it is only because of Christ's blood sacrifice that you are able to be a part of God's family. Consider it a high and lofty privilege to fellowship with such a great and royal family. When we take Communion with our fellow brothers and sisters in Christ, we are truly eating with Jesus. When we receive Holy Communion as eating with Jesus, we will be very careful not to judge anyone, especially those who sit at the table of the Lord.

> *For if we would judge ourselves, we would not be judged.* (1 Corinthians 11:31)

When we understand and act on this verse, we will be quick to judge ourselves and equally quick to forgive others. As we partake in Holy Communion, let us remember Jesus, His blood, and His body. Let us expect during this time to receive a divine transfer of healing into our bodies that will remain.

Hearing and Receiving the Word

> *Therefore He who supplies the Spirit to you and works miracles among you, does He do it by the works of the law, or by the hearing of faith?* (Galatians 3:5)

> *So then faith comes by hearing, and hearing by the word of God.*
> (Romans 10:17)

One of the ways that we can be healed is simply by hearing and receiving the Word of God. It is interesting to see people who have heard a message on healing several times, when the truth of God's Word actually dawns on them. They receive their healing. Faith will come after you continue to hear the Word of God concerning healing. Faith is like a muscle in that it has to be developed over a period of time through repeated exercise. Hearing God's Word is something that believers need to do constantly. This strengthening of our faith through hearing God's Word will make us likely candidates to receive the benefits of our Lord. The Spirit of God works miracles in our midst when we hear faith words or the word of faith. We cannot discount the power of this practice because it is effective. Faith comes when we continually and repeatedly hear the Word of God. Few individuals grasp the Word immediately. It is the practice of continuing in the Word that fortifies our understanding and makes our spirits ready for the deeper things of God.

Faith begins with hearing. An outstanding biblical example of this truth is the woman who

> The Spirit of God works miracles in our midst when we hear faith words or the word of faith.

had hemorrhaged continuously for twelve years. She had spent all of her income on physicians and medical bills in her pursuit of getting healed. Although she had endured much pain and suffering because of her mistreatment by the medical profession, her health had not gotten any better; instead, it had steadily declined. However, one day she heard a word about Jesus and His ability to heal. She believed it and acted on her faith.

> *When she heard about Jesus, she came behind Him in the crowd and touched His garment. For she said, "If only I may touch His clothes, I shall be made well." Immediately the fountain of her blood was dried up, and she felt in her body that she was healed of the affliction.* (Mark 5:27–29)

This woman's healing began when she heard about Jesus. Hearing the Word of God and of His healing nature has a therapeutic quality. That is why it is so important to guard what you hear. Be aware of negative words going into your spirit. The same way that God's Word heals, Satan's words steal, kill, and destroy.

Words of Knowledge and Wisdom

As I mentioned previously in the example of the woman who refused healing prayer, there are times when people can be healed through receiving a word of knowledge. A word of knowledge is one of the gifts of the Holy Spirit listed in 1 Corinthians 12:8–10. The word of knowledge is a divine revelation given to a person by God for a particular individual, and it unfolds the purposes and plans of God for that person's life.

Many critics claim that God does not reveal information in this manner anymore. Do not let an undiscerning person prevent you from receiving what belongs to you. Furthermore, the word of knowledge will be confirmed in you. It will not be a totally foreign word, but rather one that proves God's desire to continue the work inside you that He has already started. This word should be received as a word from the Lord.

God may also use the word of wisdom, another of the gifts of the Spirit, to communicate a reason why healing has not yet been received. The word of knowledge provides key answers to complex, problematic situations. It will identify strongholds and give solutions to destroy them so that your healing can be received and maintained.

Positively Confessing the Word

Without knowing the force of words, it is impossible to know men.   —*Confucius*

Words are, of course, the most powerful drug used by mankind. —*Rudyard Kipling*

If you wish to know the mind of a man, listen to his words.   —*Chinese Proverb*

In confession...we open our lives to the healing, reconciling, restoring, uplifting grace of Him who loves us in spite of what we are.   —*Louis Cassels*

For by your words you will be justified, and by your words you will be condemned.   —*Jesus* (Matthew 12:37)

In the chapter entitled, "Words Count," I dealt at length with the value and usage of words.

Once again, I cannot stress enough the importance of speaking what you desire on a regular basis. It would be beneficial for you to create a detailed written list of what you desire and speak it out loud several times daily. What you continually say will become what you believe. What you believe will eventually become your conviction. Your convictions will become a resident part of your character. You will always receive the manifestations of your convictions, whether they are good or bad. This entire developmental process starts with one statement. By saying "I am healed" repeatedly, you are releasing the ability of God to provide, from within His character, the nature of healing. When you confess, "I am healed," you set in motion your assigned workers to bring the necessary resources to help aid in your healing process.

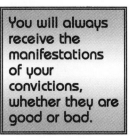

You will always receive the manifestations of your convictions, whether they are good or bad.

The power of positive confession may seem to some as unnecessary or even pointless. The person who believes this way has not reached a level in life where they have understood the spirituality of words. Your confessions create your environment. Above and beyond what anyone confesses about you is what you continue to confess about yourself.

> *I say to you, whoever says to this mountain, "Be removed and be cast into the sea," and does not doubt in his heart, but believes that those things he says will be done, he will have whatever he says. Therefore I say to you, whatever things you ask when you pray, believe that you receive them, and you will have them.* (Mark 11:23–24)

Here, the word *"says,"* as it relates to our confession, is used three times. The message that is being delivered here is that, regardless of the size of the mountain that you are endeavoring to conquer, your confession will bring possession. Confession brings possession. Possession comes when you believe that what you speak is supposed to come through for you. Regularly confess words of healing and words of faith, and expect your healing to manifest itself.

The Use of Prayer Cloths

The use of prayer cloths is another means by which people were healed biblically. The term *prayer cloth* is not found in Scripture, but the use of cloths in some form is a scriptural method.

> *Now God worked unusual miracles by the hands of Paul, so that even handkerchiefs or aprons were brought from his body to the sick, and the diseases left them and the evil spirits went out of them.*
> (Acts 19:11–12)

This may be the most unconventional practice employed by people in the body of Christ. As with any workable method, excesses and misuses are always potential factors. Without question, there have been abuses with prayer cloths. However, the abuses need to be corrected rather than discarding the method. For far too long, the body of Christ has thrown out scriptural means of spiritual healing because of one person's excesses.

> For far too long, the body of Christ has thrown out scriptural means of spiritual healing because of one person's excesses.

Some theologians have argued that methods of this kind can lead hopeful individuals into despair and depression. They consider such an approach to be misleading and unfruitful. Although that argument may have validity from one perspective, consider the various other points of view that we can take. There is the possibility of God's using this method to heal. He has done it before, and surely He can do it again. We cannot afford, by our human logic, to exclude God from any situation just to accommodate our theological posturing.

There are legitimate street vendors on the sidewalks of New York City selling goods for profit honestly. There are also unregulated, unregistered, crooked peddlers on the streets of New York City, preying on naive tourists in order to exchange inferior goods and supplies for cash. Should we rule out spending our hard-earned dollars in New York City because of the potential of being ripped off by a shyster posing as a legitimate salesperson? Absolutely not! However, we need to be more careful to deal with those who can prove their legitimacy. In the same manner, the burden remains on the believer to be discerning enough to know who is operating under the power of the Anointed One.

> The burden remains on the believer to be discerning enough to know who is operating under the power of the Anointed One.

Some theologians would argue that this scriptural reference should not stand because it can be found only in one place in Scripture. It is true that the only place in the Bible that we can find the use of prayer cloths is found in Acts 19:11–12. Yet, there is another incident in which cloth and clothing were used as the conduit for the healing power of God.

> *And suddenly, a woman who had a flow of blood for twelve years came from behind and touched the hem of His garment. For she said to herself, "If only I may touch His garment, I shall be made well." But Jesus turned around, and when He saw her He said, "Be of good cheer, daughter; your faith has made you well." And the woman was made well from that hour.* (Matthew 9:20–22)

The clothing that was worn by Jesus was capable of transmitting the flow of the power of God. I recognize that the cloth itself was powerless. From the examples of Paul and Jesus, it appears that clothing has the capacity to take on the nature of the person who wears it. So since Jesus, the Anointed One, wears clothes, then His clothes are also anointed with His anointing.

I do believe that God can use anything to bring glory to His name. All of our possessions belong to God. If we yield our possessions to Him, He will empower our "stuff" to assist in the work of the ministry. Handkerchiefs and apron cloths were used to bring healing. The hem of Jesus' garment was used to bring healing. What God did then, He can and will do in a greater measure now. Although this means of healing may unsettle some rigidly held beliefs, it may also serve the believer well in bringing healing and restoration.

Prayer and Fasting

> *Rejoice always, pray without ceasing, in everything give thanks; for this is the will of God in Christ Jesus for you.* (1 Thessalonians 5:16–18)

> *Confess your trespasses to one another, and pray for one another, that you may be healed. The effective, fervent prayer of a righteous man avails much.* (James 5:16)

> *Watch therefore, and pray always that you may be counted worthy to escape all these things that will come to pass, and to stand before the Son of Man.* (Luke 21:36)

> *So Abraham prayed to God; and God healed Abimelech, his wife, and his female servants. Then they bore children.*
> (Genesis 20:17)

The Word of God has much to say about prayer. Prayer is the most essential element of our life in Christ. As humans we need oxygenated air in order to breathe and live. Such is the case with us as spiritual beings. Our spirits cannot live without prayer.

Prayer is the vehicle of communication between God and mankind. Prayer does not mean that we are doing all the talking; it isn't a monologue. Rather, prayer suggests a dialogue between two people who are in a love affair. What we want God to know, we say to Him. In the same way, when God wants to communicate a message to us, He speaks it into our spirits. Because prayer is a dialogue, much listening and quiet time is required when we pray.

> Because prayer is a dialogue, much listening and quiet time is required when we pray.

God is the supreme, strong One in this relationship, the Supplier of all of our needs. Therefore, when we pray, we pray with an overwhelming confidence that the One to whom we pray has more than enough in Him to heal us. The enemy has convinced many believers that prayer is not very important. This deception has caused many casualties in the body of Christ. Prayer is one of our greatest weapons against the enemy. It is our greatest weapon in pulling down the enemy's strongholds.

> *For the weapons of our warfare are not*
> *carnal but mighty in God for pulling down*
> *strongholds.* (2 Corinthians 10:4)

Perhaps the mightiest weapon Christians have is prayer. This weapon is available for our use at all times, yet many believers rarely access its power. Every human need that exists can be properly dealt with in prayer.

Sickness and disease can be categorized with other evils of society, such as racism, sexism, and classism. Their roots are all evil. All of these evils can be discussed for our enlightenment. However, they will never go away because we teach or preach about them. Of course, as kingdom citizens we must continue to teach and educate the believers of the tricks, schemes, and plans of the enemy. Teaching on these themes is of much value. Still, these evils will never go away until concentrated, united prayer takes place.

God has shown us in His Word that major results occur when we pray. Nations are changed and look to God for salvation when we pray. Famine in the land turns to abundance of agricultural harvest when we pray. Poverty and lack are reversed when we pray, receive instruction from Him, and make the necessary adjustments. The wrath of God is quieted when we pray.

People are healed when we pray. Abraham prayed and God healed Abimelech, his wife, and his servants. Hezekiah prayed and God continued his life for fifteen years. Throughout the ages God has responded to the prayers of His people concerning healing.

Unfortunately, in our microwave society, we expect to pray once and forget it. This method may work at times, but not always. The intensity of the trial may determine the intensity of the prayer and its duration. While God can do anything, we must recognize His

> The intensity of the trial may determine the intensity of the prayer and its duration.

timing. In His timing, He allows us to prepare ourselves for what He desires us to have.

There are some who, if healed by God, would neither thank Him nor serve Him. The Lord knows the whole range of human behavior and specifically how each of us would act in any given situation.

> *Now He who searches the hearts knows what the mind of the Spirit is, because He makes intercession for the saints according to the will of God.* (Romans 8:27)

In His love and mercy, God will give us time to correct our behavior, so that when the blessing comes, it will not serve as a curse to us.

Prayer is the lost art of the saints. In the final days before Christ returns, prayer will be restored to the body of Christ in its fullness. We will see prayer conventions and prayer meetings with overflowing numbers of people attending them. The mature believer recognizes the dire need for prayer.

Prayer alone can heal the body. In his epistle James referred to prayer as it relates to the sick:

*And the prayer of faith will save the sick,
and the Lord will raise him up. And if he
has committed sins, he will be forgiven.*
(James 5:15)

James said that the prayer of faith is one that will save the sick. Prayer has within it all of the ingredients for success as God defines success. The enemy will use every means possible to keep believers from praying. He knows better than we often do how powerful we become through concentrated and continual prayer. Prayer works!

> Prayer has within it all of the ingredients for success as God defines success.

The Bible also discloses an even more avoided, yet needed, discipline called fasting. Fasting is defined as abstaining from food. When we fast, we become better. Unlike prayer, fasting is not for God. While prayer delights God through our communion and fellowship with Him, fasting is generally self-centered. Prayer is God-centered. The purpose for fasting is to discipline our flesh so much that we can hear clearly from God.

The Pharisees made fasting a religious ritual devoid of meaning. They wanted God to applaud them for their abstinence from foods. God could not give them any applause because it did not affect Him. If you fast to get God's approval, it is a futile effort, and it should properly be termed starvation, not fasting. You cannot use fasting as a means of getting God's attention so that He will do what you desire. He will not heal you just because you fasted. When you fast, however, you will hear from Him as to the plan that He has prepared for your healing.

Hearing God's voice means everything. Because prayer is a dialogue, hearing from Him is necessary in communicating. Fasting will take us away from the world's system long enough to hear from God. There are some people who pray regularly, yet never hear from God. They need to fast. If you are not hearing what God is speaking to you, there is something in your life that is cluttering the receiver in your

> If you are not hearing what God is speaking to you, there is something in your life that is cluttering the receiver in your spirit.

spirit. Fasting will help you to identify exactly what that something is.

Fasting is a spiritual discipline, practiced by the prophets and patriarchs of old. Jesus himself fasted in the wilderness. Of course, Jesus was not fasting to become more spiritual, but rather to hear clearly what the Father had to say.

There will be times when the sickness that you encounter will be one of great demonic association. This close demonic connection to your sickness may call for you to fast and pray.

When the disciples were confronted by a child with a deaf and dumb spirit, they could not cast the spirit out of the child. This spirit was connected with demons. This would require more discipline than prayer alone.

> So He said to them, "This kind can come out by nothing but prayer and fasting."
> (Mark 9:29)

Again, fasting for the disciples would have caused their hearing to be keen enough to hear directions from God. Jesus was constantly hearing from God because He fasted and prayed on a continual basis. Jesus commanded the spirit to come out of the child. The spirit came out of him.

The child appeared to be lifeless. Jesus then touched the child, and the child regained life and strength.

Afterward, the disciples asked Jesus in a private session, "Why couldn't we do what You did?" Jesus' response was and is, for all who desire to see mighty things happen through your life:

Fast and pray!

chapter eight

Atmosphere Is Everything

In this chapter we will cover a theme that has not been dealt with to my knowledge in a written format. This theme is the atmosphere and the environment that are conducive for healing to occur. While there are not many Scriptures that deal specifically with the atmosphere for healing, we do have a scriptural basis for the atmosphere that must be present in order for God to show up.

The Bible says,

> *Let all things be done decently and in order.* (1 Corinthians 14:40)

This verse lets us know that God expects order in all things. The church has needed to repent in this area. We have lost godly order in many situations. Because order is lacking in many churches, God does not show himself mighty, and people remain sick. Chaos and confusion rather than power and demonstration of the Lord characterize many Sunday morning services.

> *For God is not the author of confusion but of peace, as in all the churches of the saints.* (1 Corinthians 14:33)

There must be an atmosphere that God requires for us to get favorable results all of the time.

The Congregation

Anytime people congregate to worship together, whether in a church or a hotel or a hall or even a coliseum, the enemy will cause distractions and annoyances to interrupt the flow of the anointing. At times when I am teaching on Sunday morning, children may become excessively noisy. When the ushers politely ask the parents to control their children, often parents become offended and abruptly leave the service. Although drinking and eating are prohibited during services, people sometimes fail to follow these rules. There are times when people, children and adults alike, find the need to perform like clowns in the house of the Lord. They crack jokes. They hold conversations with one another. They fail to reverence and recognize the presence of the King in our midst. These are just a few of the tools that the enemy uses to distract our attention away from the Anointed One.

When we fall prey to the distractions of the enemy, we lose more than we ever thought we would have lost. When we offend the Holy Spirit by our behavior and attitudes, He leaves grieved and will not return unless repentance is heartfelt and announced. It is the work of the Holy Spirit of Christ, the Anointed One, to bring healing to us. When we offend Him, we lose the opportunity of being healed at that time.

> *And do not grieve the Holy Spirit of God, by whom you were sealed for the day of redemption.* (Ephesians 4:30)

When we congregate to worship the Christ, we must have a central focus of purpose and meaning. We are not congregating to make friends.

We are not congregating to network or to make contacts for our own selfish purposes. We are there for the express purpose of praising the Lord for His infinite worth.

In such an environment where God is being righteously praised, His Spirit will literally overtake the worshipper. When this occurs, whatever has ailed you will be gone, for God's presence is far greater than our problems. This is why God is said to live within our praises. When we praise and worship God, He steps into our lives and will not leave. As long as the spirit of praise dwells in you, He will permanently dwell there, too.

> *But You are holy, enthroned in the praises of Israel.* (Psalm 22:3)

Where order and praise connect is the point of supernatural manifestation. In order for this power to be released, order must be present. The atmosphere needs to be just right to produce the glory of God. That production of His glory begins in us. We are glory producers.

Because the environment during a healing service is a critical issue, many things cannot be tolerated. Lives are at stake. Spirits are waiting to be born again. The enemy would do anything in his power to interrupt what God has planned for the service. In light of this, the following things must be considered and implemented in order to create a successful environment for healing and wholeness. Children must be well-behaved and quiet. They cannot make outbursts, be fidgety, or cause any distraction that will draw anyone's attention away from the Word of God and God Himself. Because of their level of immaturity, infants and toddlers lack understanding and cannot be properly controlled during a healing and worship service. Crying and cooing can be major distractions during the presentation of God's Word. Talking in general is disrespectful and should not be allowed in the house of the Lord. The only talking that should be permitted is talking to the Lord or affirming what the minister is preaching by simply saying, "Amen." Even this must be done in a decent manner and not in a manner to draw attention to oneself. Walking back and forth and excessive movement are other major distractions that must be kept to an absolute minimum.

Speaking in other tongues at an inappropriate time is one of the greatest distractions during a healing service. Solomon expressed the important of recognizing timing: *"To everything there is a season, a time for every purpose under heaven"* (Ecclesiastes 3:1). There is a time to speak in tongues and a time to refrain from speaking in tongues. When the presence of the Lord is present to heal, God's people need to hear Him, not you. Your voice will only become a competition to God's voice. Since you are not fair competition for God, He will simply leave. When He leaves, someone has missed an opportunity to be free because of your unrestrained zeal. Be careful not to be zealous without using knowledge.

All of these conditions are set forth only to provide an environment worthy of God's presence. To those who are offended by the unacceptable behaviors I have outlined, I pray that God will open your eyes and give you understanding. While the world maintains its order in the justice system, the church must lead the world by example in sacred respect for the things of God.

Music and Instruments

I believe that music has healing attributes because it originates in God. Music has the capacity to minister to the soul and spirit. Because of the high potential of music, music in the healing service must be carefully and prayerfully selected. This area is one that can very easily be a hindrance to entering into the presence of the Lord.

Now, I am in no way implying that one style of music is more meritorious to God than another style. The Lord loves the vibrant, unrestrained Davidic praises of the Church of God in Christ. He also loves the folk-styled deep worship of the Vineyard Fellowship with its heavy guitar influences. God loves the contributions of Don Moen and the Integrity Music Group, who have led in fulfilling God's mandate of singing a new song unto the Lord. The formal and liturgical music traditions of the Catholics and Episcopalians are rich in history and robust in sound. They also represent a facet of God that should not be neglected. The more prophetic music has ushered in a whole new way of ministering to the Lord— singing forth what God speaks through you. The music of the Messianic Jews brings back the flavor of the sound of the temple in Jerusalem. This sound is one of my personal favorites, but as the younger generation says, "It's all good."

I believe that the varied music styles in the church only reveal the many characteristics of God. Sometimes we dance with the Lord, at other times we cry with God. Often we laugh in the presence of God with great joy and gladness. However, there are times when He can barely hear us above the din because the timing calls for stillness and quietness in the presence of the Lord. God uses all of these praise and worship forms to bring glory to His name.

The real concern that I am voicing deals with God's timing and our sensitivity to the Holy Spirit. There is a time and place for everything. When we enter into holy worship, it is not the time to break out in a dance. This will only disturb the flow of His presence. God does not dislike dancing. His Word declares that young and old people should go forth in the dance. But dancing will interrupt His order if He is calling for quietness.

The underlying theme here is obeying God. Right now you may be thinking, *Pastor Aaron, what if I do not know what God is saying?* Then you ought to obey the instruction of whoever is leading the praise and worship service. The presence of God connects when God sees order.

The order that God is looking for is that of unity.

> *Behold, how good and how pleasant it is for brethren to dwell together in unity! It is like the precious oil upon the head, running down on the beard, the beard of Aaron, running down on the edge of his garments. It is like the dew of Hermon, descending upon the mountains of Zion; for there the LORD commanded the blessing; life forevermore.* (Psalm 133:1–3)

Blessings will not come until we are first unified. I believe that the reason why there was such a glorious spiritual outpouring in the Upper Room at Pentecost (see Acts 2) is because of the oneness, the unity, that was present.

*When the Day of Pentecost had fully come,
they were all with one accord in one place.*
(Acts 2:1)

God dwells in the unified church. God hates discord and disorder and confusion. In such an environment, nothing of value gets accomplished.

In the healing service, everyone needs to be in one accord with the music. Even if you do not particularly care for the style, you need to recognize that it is not about style but about purpose. God has purposed someone to be born again during that service. God has purposed for someone to be healed. He has purposed for someone to be set free and delivered from addiction. His purpose should always be more important than our tastes and preferences.

Jesus Himself recognized the purpose factor and submitted to the higher will of His Father. Although it would be painful for Him to die an innocent death, He still submitted.

*He went a little farther and fell on His
face, and prayed, saying, "O My Father, if
it is possible, let this cup pass from Me;
nevertheless, not as I will, but as You
will."* (Matthew 26:39)

In His model for prayer, Jesus confirmed this stand:

*Your kingdom come. Your will be done on
earth as it is in heaven.* (Matthew 6:10)

It is God's will for us to be so unified that our oneness creates an inviting atmosphere for miracles, signs, and wonders.

Knowing these things, we must realize that in the worship service our desire should be to create an atmosphere that pleases God, not necessarily our personal tastes. All instruments are welcome during the service to create the right mood. Some instruments, however, are appropriate for certain times. A rock guitar sound during a solemn moment of focusing on God's goodness would be highly offensive to the Holy Spirit. The timing is wrong.

The lyrics in the music should be in direct alignment with what we are believing God to do. During a healing service, it is out of place to sing the song, "I'll Fly Away." Why would anyone sing about leaving this earthly realm while believing God to heal his body? The words of the music should be in direct relationship to healing and God's holy presence.

There is also a time to rejoice with vivacity. After someone has received healing, it is only reasonable for the person to be extremely excited. Not long ago, during a healing service that was being conducted by a prominent minister, I witnessed an amazing miracle. There was a man who was probably in his early forties and who had never seen anything before. He was totally blind. During the message that the minister gave, this brother released his faith for healing. The minister taught on the story of the person who was born blind and received his sight. (See John 9.) This brother believed that if God did it before, He could do it again. He received his healing during the service. When he discovered that he could see, he got so excited that he began running around the coliseum, shouting with overwhelming excitement.

Some ministers would attempt to calm this brother down, claiming that he was being too emotional. This type of criticism, in my estimation, is unfair and unreasonable. If you had gone blind and God had just restored your sight, would you—could you—be quiet and dignified? I know I couldn't! I would be dancing and shouting praises to God.

The central point I am trying to make is that the service belongs to the Lord. Since the Lord is ultimately in control, we must worship and praise Him as He desires.

God is Spirit, and those who worship Him must worship in spirit and truth.
(John 4:24)

The Atmosphere in the Hospital and the Home

Some of the most difficult places that I have had to pray for the sick are in convalescent homes, hospitals, and personal residences. Without question, God can do anything. However, we often limit God by our surroundings. In other words, the atmosphere that we create will either usher in the presence of God or drive His presence far from our dwellings.

> The atmosphere that we create will either usher in the presence of God or drive His presence far from our dwellings.

I have been in several hospitals to visit people who were dying with cancer. They claimed to be standing in faith for their healing. Yet I could not help but notice what they were watching on television. In one situation with a critically ill person, the movie *Dirty Dancing* was airing. After it was over, a videocassette of *Sleeping with the Enemy* was ready to be slipped into the VCR. It is incomprehensible to me why people would feed their spirits with anything that is not spiritual at such a crucial time. When I am asked to pray, it is always difficult for me to filter through all of the spiritual interference that is so apparent in the atmosphere.

Whether at home or in the hospital, sick people who are believing that God will heal them should consciously quarantine themselves from anything that is not spiritual. The sick believer should have a planned day of routine spiritual occurrences. If the person is too sick to pray or read the Word of God, then their loved ones ought to make that house or hospital room just right for the presence of the Lord to dwell in.

These are some things that anyone who is bedridden should do. First, take no phone calls. The phone has a way of becoming a carnal connection to gossip and backbiting. In most cases, phone conversations will not strengthen you, but rather add to your already weak state. Pastors or ministers may call in the event that they cannot come to visit personally. Even in this case, people must be willing to inform the minister that they are in the need of prayer, not negative remarks. Another thing that you must do is to play cassettes or videos with teaching about healing throughout the entire course of the day. If you have compact discs of inspirational music, play those continuously. What you are doing is creating an environment for God.

Just as doctors, depending on their musical tastes, may listen to classical or jazz music as they perform surgery, God also wants the sound of healing to be in the room where He will perform His mighty acts. The environment in a hospital is already filled with sickness and disease. You must be cautious not to facilitate the spirit of sickness by disregarding negative influences. Not one moment of any day should there be an absence of the sound of healing in your midst. Even when you are sleeping, healing sounds should be playing softly, whether teaching or music. Faith comes by hearing the Word of God. By continuously listening to the Word, you will not have one moment where fear or doubt can enter in, since you will be in a constant arena of faith.

> By continuously listening to the Word, you will not have one moment where fear or doubt can enter in, since you will be in a constant arena of faith.

The Company You Keep, the Advice You Take

You must also screen your visitors. There are some people, including family members, who just are not good company to be around when you are in such a state. They will make ridiculous remarks such as, "It was good knowing you," and "Look at the bright side; at least you'll see Jesus soon." You do not need anyone like that around you. Select your company carefully. If at all possible, try to surround yourself with people of faith at all times. Post signs on the wall wherever you are of passages in God's Word on healing.

Follow your physician's advice, especially as it relates to your diet. Proper diet is very important for your healing process to manifest itself. In addition, you must get a lot of sleep. During this time your body will begin to heal itself. Over-exhaustion and sleeplessness will only aggravate your present condition. Also, because you are under medical care, God expects that you will obey your caretaker as long as the provision is within the guidelines of your personal convictions and God's Word.

> **Your spirit of obedience will help to create an atmosphere of healing.**

Your spirit of obedience will help to create an atmosphere of healing. Get rid of all secular music. Don't watch any secular programming or movies. Ban the negative attitudes and speech of other people, and eliminate them in yourself. Allow nothing in your life unless it is bathed in faith.

> *And again He entered Capernaum after some days, and it was heard that He was in the house. Immediately many gathered together, so that there was no longer room to receive them, not even near the door. And He preached the word to them. Then they came to Him, bringing a paralytic who was carried by four men. And when they could not come near Him because of the crowd, they uncovered the roof where He was. So when they had broken through, they let down the bed on which the paralytic was lying. When Jesus saw their faith, He said to the paralytic, "Son, your sins are forgiven you."* (Mark 2:1–5)

Jesus will always enter a house or a room of faith and heal the sick. In this passage in Mark, Jesus was preaching the Word to a crowd gathered in Simon Peter's house, where Jesus stayed whenever He came to Capernaum. This paralytic man had some great friends who were full of faith. They had so much faith that even though the house was full of people, they were determined to get their friend inside where Jesus was. Not only was there faith inside the house, but faith was also working outside the house. Jesus saw the faith of this paralytic man's friends. Jesus, because of the atmosphere of faith, responded in healing toward

Faith-filled atmospheres always produce miracles.

the paralytic. Faith-filled atmospheres always produce miracles.

The Right Church

The church that you attend has much to do with your physical condition. While some may not believe this to be true, it has more validity than you might ever realize. Take an inventory of just how many people in your local congregation are sick. You would be amazed at the sickness and disease that is allowed to thrive in the churches in the world. From what we have learned, it seems that all churches are to be centers of healing. Sadly, that is not the actual case.

A church will produce only what it sows. If the pastor is continually sick and confessing sickness, you have little chance of staying healthy and free of disease. You can be no more than what your leadership is feeding you by words and example. You may ask, "Are you telling me to leave my church, Pastor Aaron?" Please understand that I am not telling you to do anything. The only thing I will say is that you need to ask the Holy Spirit to connect you to the place of your destiny, the place of your calling. Only in this place will you prosper and be in health. You will know when God is speaking.

You will be able to distinguish an unstable church-hopping tendency in yourself from the Lord's leading. Church-hoppers are never satisfied anywhere. They find fault no matter where they go. People who are led by God will leave a church peacefully. Once believers connect with the healing ministry that God called them to, they will foresee a future of sowing and growing with that ministry. It is crucial that you are in the proper place of godly assignment.

> Once believers connect with the healing ministry that God called them to, they will foresee a future of sowing and growing with that ministry.

I have been to several churches where the pastor and his parishioners suffer from cancer and other chronic diseases. These sickly traits characterize this type of ministry. Often, the ministry is known in the city to be a sick church. When a church has a disproportionate number of physically unhealthy people, there is a direct connection to a lack of spiritual healthiness and a lack of solid biblical teaching.

If a church does not preach and practice healing, then it is not a healing church. I have heard many pastors deliver messages on healing, concentrating on what Jesus did. Merely preaching about the healing acts of Jesus does not make a local body a healing church. What does makes it a healing church is the ongoing demonstration of Jesus' ministry and miracles. Healing the sick ought to be a regular occurrence in every church. Every church in the world needs to be a healing church because the world needs healing. Spiritual, physical, emotional, and mental healing is the business of the church.

Sowing Seeds of Health

The principle that governs the law of return in the kingdom of God is called the law of seedtime and harvest.

> *While the earth remains, seedtime and harvest, cold and heat, winter and summer, and day and night shall not cease.*
> (Genesis 8:22)

As long as this planet exists, the principle of seedtime and harvest will never cease. Whatever people sow, whether good or bad, that is exactly what they will reap. This law cannot change. This same law works in local assemblies around the world. If you sow seeds of healing messages and seeds of praying for the sick to be healed, you will reap a healthy church. If you neglect to sow seeds of healing and pray for the sick only occasionally, you will eventually have as many funerals as you do water baptisms.

A healing church cannot minister on the topic of healing once a year and expect favorable results. It must be one of the constant themes of the ministry. The minister must continually sow healing. It is not what you do once in a while that pro-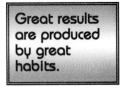duces great results. Great results are produced by great habits. Healing must be the habit of your church.

In the church I pastor, nearly every member is experiencing great health. Just because they are healthy is no reason for me to stop preaching, teaching, and practicing spiritual healing. I will continue to sow healing seeds so our ministry and congregation will continue to reap healing. If your church does not actively preach, teach, and practice healing, you are not in the right church to be healed. The church in which the Lord Jesus Christ visits and performs miracles is the church whose members are so desperate that they will tear the roof off the church just to get a friend healed. God is looking for a church that operates in faith. God desires to dwell there, for that is the atmosphere that was created especially for Him.

Be creative, and set the stage for your healing.

chapter nine

Hindrances to Healing

While we have covered some hindrances to healing in previous chapters, there are still three major barriers that we need to discuss in order to give substance and completeness to this work on healing. These three hindrances can prevent you not only from receiving healing, but also from receiving any good thing from the Lord.

Unforgiveness

God has a big eraser.　　　　*—Billy Zeoli*

Only the brave know how to forgive; it is the most refined and generous pitch of virtue human nature can arrive at.
—Laurence Sterne

Forgiveness is God's command.
—Martin Luther

The weak can never forgive. Forgiveness is the attribute of the strong.
—Mahatma Gandhi

Forgive yourself for your faults and your mistakes and move on.　　*—Les Brown*

The first hindrance to healing is unforgiveness. Unforgiveness is a nasty word. It is especially distasteful in the ranks of professing believers. When an individual refuses to forgive another person, that unforgiving individual carries not only his own sin, but also the sin of the person whom he does not release. The act of forgiveness releases both the offender and the one who was offended.

What forgiveness does for the one who offers it is far more valuable than what it does for the one who receives it. One reason is that there are God-given universal principles in operation continuously. With any act of forgiveness, the law of sowing and reaping is triggered, accompanied by the truth that *"it is more blessed to give than to receive"* (Acts 20:35).

One of the reasons that it is more blessed to give forgiveness than to receive forgiveness because the forgiver is elevated to a higher position in the kingdom. This position is called the seat of humility. While in this seat, the Lord continues to build

Unforgiveness clogs the flow of kingdom power into the believer's life.

you up with blessings and provision. Unforgiveness blocks the entire process, causing potential blessings to stop reaching you. God does not bless indwelling, unrepented sin. Unforgiveness is sin. Unforgiveness clogs the flow of kingdom power into the believer's life.

What has come to be known as the Lord's Prayer has as much to say about forgiveness as it does about the kingdom of God.

> *...And forgive us our debts, as we forgive our debtors. And do not lead us into temptation, but deliver us from the evil one. For Yours is the kingdom and the power and the glory forever. Amen.* (Matthew 6:12–13)

After the Model Prayer, Jesus continued teaching his disciples about the importance of forgiveness.

> *For if you forgive men their trespasses, your heavenly Father will also forgive you. But if you do not forgive men their trespasses, neither will your Father forgive your trespasses.* (Matthew 6:14–15)

This passage is powerful. It lets us know that if we refuse to forgive others, God will not forgive us either. These verses seem to reveal that we have considerable control over the measure by which God forgives us. If we forgive much, then God will forgive us much. If we forgive little, God will forgive us little. If we do not forgive, neither will God forgive us.

Millions of people in this world are sick right now because they refuse to forgive family and friends of wrongdoings from many years ago. They have lived with the scars and wounds of the offender. In many cases the offender moved on long ago, but the sick person has steadfastly refused to release the offense and the offender. Yet those who harbor unforgiveness often still believe that God is obligated to forgive them when they trespass against Him.

It always makes me wonder when I hear a young single woman declare, "If my husband-to-be ever cheats on me, I could never forgive him." Expressions such as this lead me to speculate about her underlying attitudes. This woman has already planned not to forgive in the event that something as tragic as infidelity occurs within the bonds of marriage. However, this same woman may be fornicating with the prospective husband-to-be, yet feel no remorse about her sin in the eyes of God Almighty. It is evident that she expects God to forgive her. She is breaking His law and commandment. Although she expects God to forgive her, she has predetermined in her heart not to forgive her husband in the event that he sins.

Sin is sin. The husband would not be justified in the event of his adultery. However, neither is she justified in purposing to commit an act that violates her covenant with God. Unfortunately, this is the mindset of most people, even Christians. "God, forgive me for my sin, but I am not going to forgive him for his sin."

Our unforgiveness grieves God far more than the sins we commit. Jesus shed His blood to cover our sins. He gave His absolute best to redeem us from sin. God hurts in ways we do not understand. He grieves with great intensity when He sees His children withholding forgiveness in light of how much He has forgiven us. This devilish trait of unforgiveness will stop the flow of healing in your life.

> **This devilish trait of unforgiveness will stop the flow of healing in your life.**

Right now, say this prayer with me:

Father, in the name of the Lord Jesus Christ, I pray that you will forgive me of the sin of unforgiveness. I realize that I am in no position now nor will I ever be in a position to withhold forgiveness from anyone. I am now aware that when I forgive, I open my spirit to receive Your unconditional love and forgiveness. When I do not forgive, I know it grieves You because I limit Your ability to prosper me as You so desire.

From this moment on, I renounce the spirit of unforgiveness and cast it out of my life, never to return again. Not only will I forgive, but I will also seek opportunities to forgive.

Father, I thank You for hearing me, forgiving me, and cleansing me. Amen.

Disobedience

Unwavering obedience to the true principles we learn will assure us spiritual survival. —*Anonymous*

The next barrier to your healing is disobedience. While much of modern theology has made disobedience a trivial matter in the eyes of man, it is still crucial in the eyes of the Lord. God expects us to obey Him. When we willfully and consciously disobey Him, we are dishonoring Him. We should not expect God's healing power to be evident in our lives if we disregard everything He instructs us to do. Jesus let us know that if we love God, we will obey Him by keeping His commandments: *"If you love Me, keep My commandments"* (John 14:15).

> We should not expect God's healing power to be evident in our lives if we disregard everything He instructs us to do.

Disobedience is rebellion against God's Word. God considers disobedience as evil and as serpentine as the sin of witchcraft.

For rebellion is as the sin of witchcraft, and stubbornness is as iniquity and idolatry. Because you have rejected the word of the LORD, He also has rejected you from being king. (1 Samuel 15:23)

God cannot prosper you in your disobedience. In Deuteronomy 28:15–68, we see a graphically detailed outline of the curse that comes upon people when they choose to live in a state of disobedience to God. Prior to that passage, we see only fourteen verses that deal with the blessings associated with obedience. Why would God list more curses than blessings? After all, isn't God a God of blessings? Doesn't He desire prosperity for us? God does want us to prosper, but our choices and attitudes determine what comes into our lives. When we willfully choose to disobey God, we are also opting to receive everything that goes with that choice. However, if we repent, then *"He is faithful and just to forgive us our sins and to cleanse us from all unrighteousness"* (1 John 1:9).

God is not a vindictive God. God is not seeking revenge because we have disobeyed Him. In fact, it hurts God greatly when we disobey Him, not because of the act itself, but because it limits the extent to which He can bless us. God is saying, "I want to heal you, but the spirit of disobedience prohibits me from making the deposit of healing." It is as if you had closed a banking account, yet you are still trying to make deposits in the account. It is absurd to think that you can make a deposit in a closed account. Likewise, we close our heavenly bank accounts with God when we live in perpetual disobedience, but we reopen them for heavenly transactions when we repent and walk in obedience to God's Word.

> We close our heavenly bank accounts with God when we live in perpetual disobedience, but we reopen them for heavenly transactions when we repent and walk in obedience to God's Word.

God is not trying to zap us for every wrong thing that we do. That is not His purpose. I personally believe that He does not keep a track record of our sins. I do believe that He does keep our rate of repentance on record.

As we understand and learn more about obedience toward God and His Word, we will recognize that our obedience is an act of love for God. Obedience will not be painful drudgery for us when it becomes a natural response out of the love we have for Christ.

> *"If you are willing and obedient, you shall eat the good of the land; but if you refuse and rebel, you shall be devoured by the sword"; for the mouth of the LORD has spoken.* (Isaiah 1:19–20)

Double-Mindedness

> *If any of you lacks wisdom, let him ask of God, who gives to all liberally and without reproach, and it will be given to him. But let him ask in faith, with no doubting, for he who doubts is like a wave of the sea driven and tossed by the wind. For let not that man suppose that he will receive anything from the Lord; he is a double-minded man, unstable in all his ways.* (James 1:5–8)

The third major hindrance to healing is double-mindedness, which means your mindset is not set at all, because it vacillates between two different viewpoints. Sometimes you believe it is God's will to heal you; other times you believe that God is trying to teach you a lesson through sickness. One day you believe God wants you to be financially prosperous; the next day you receive a call from a creditor demanding payment, and you are sure that you are going to be poor for the rest of your life. The Bible tells us that people with this spirit of double-mindedness are unstable in all of their ways.

Take note of people who have a double confession. They will display instability in many areas of their lives. Often these people cannot commit to anything. They leave one church and go to another. They can never seem to keep a job. They drop out of school a few weeks after registration. They are unstable. These individuals try to please everybody, yet they are not faithful to anyone.

This condition is usually connected with mental health issues. Like many drug addicts, double-minded people are in constant denial of their state. They are extremely afraid of true commitment because true commitment will only help to cure their mental problems.

The Bible says that the double-minded person should not expect to receive anything from the Lord.

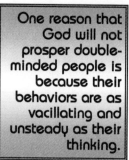
One reason that God will not prosper double-minded people is because their behaviors are as vacillating and unsteady as their thinking.

One reason that God will not prosper double-minded people is because their behaviors are as vacillating and unsteady as their thinking. Their prayer lives are extremely inconsistent. Although they claim to love God, they are poor examples of loyalty to Him. These people would only misappropriate God's blessings if given to them.

It would be ridiculous for any woman to believe that she will win the Miss America pageant if she has not entered the contest. Likewise, double-minded people have not even entered the arena of walking by faith, so it is just as absurd for them to expect anything from God. Until double-minded people have been set free from their debilitating state of mind, they will never receive their healing. Their thought patterns will always keep them from receiving God's best for their lives.

Whether you are dealing with a spirit of unforgiveness, a spirit of disobedience, or a spirit of double-mindedness, you can be set free through the power of the Lord Jesus Christ. These hindrances do not have to have a constant hold on your life. They have held you back far too long. It is time to get free.

If you really want to be free of these hindrances, please pray this prayer right now:

> Father, I confess to You that I have been unforgiving, disobedient, and double-minded. I ask Your forgiveness for having allowed these areas of sinful behavior to develop in my life and to become strongholds over me.
>
> In the name of the Lord Jesus Christ, I renounce any spirit that is not of God that has gained any place in my life, and I command it to let loose of me and depart from my life now.
>
> Lord, I thank You that You have heard me, that You have forgiven me, and that You have set me free from their grip on my spirit and mind. I confess that right now I am free from any hindrances. In Jesus' name. Amen.

chapter ten

Maintaining Your Healing

As we wrap up this subject, there is one vital area of healing that we still must deal with. We need to learn how to maintain our health properly. Through the Word of God and the power of Christ, the Anointed One, we have easy access to healing. Unfortunately, just as quickly as we receive our healing, we can lose it.

Through the years as I have delved into the spiritual aspects of healing, I have also discovered that there are measures we can undertake in the natural realm that complement the spiritual elements we have already discussed. I want to offer you several practical steps that will help to insure that the enemy never again gains the advantage in relationship to our health and healing. We will forever close the door to the enemy of sickness and premature death.

Hosea once declared, *"My people are destroyed for lack of knowledge"* (Hosea 4:6). Solomon said, *"Wisdom is the principal thing; therefore get wisdom. And in all your getting, get understanding"* (Proverbs 4:7). My intention in writing this book has been to provide you with strong defenses against the enemy when he confronts you with sickness.

Wisdom is a defense. You will need spiritual and natural wisdom in order to walk consistently in divine health. This wisdom will provoke you to make choices that may be culturally uncomfortable for you. You need to recognize that your health and well-being are of far greater value to you than your cultural preferences. Plainly stated, there are some crucial choices that you will need to make in order to sustain the healing that you have received. You must begin to change your thoughts concerning the importance of diet, rest, and exercise.

> You will need spiritual and natural wisdom in order to walk consistently in divine health.

Or do you not know that your body is the temple of the Holy Spirit who is in you, whom you have from God, and you are not your own? (1 Corinthians 6:19)

In light of this thought-provoking question posed by Paul, we need to realize that the natural steps we take to care for our physical bodies have spiritual implications. If you are born again, the Holy Spirit now dwells in your bodily temple, and it's up to you to do the housekeeping.

If you rented a vehicle, would you blow up the transmission, put water in the gasoline tank, crash the car, and tear the seats up with razors? Of course not! You would be held accountable to the rental agency for the damages. It is not your car. It belongs to someone else. You must treat it with respect if you ever want to rent a vehicle again. This idea is analogous to the relationship between God and our bodies. Our bodies belong to Him. The way we treat our bodies now will determine what God blesses us with in the future.

In the United States, we are in desperate need of dietary changes. More people die today of degenerative diseases than at any other time in the history of this nation. Most Americans ingest enormous amounts of processed foods, unnatural sugars, fats, and "foods" that have no nutritional value. This improper diet has made us a sickly nation. We must change now. Let us look at the things that we need to do in order to regain and maintain our health.

Drink Plenty of Water

You must drink lots of water on a daily basis. The human body is composed of more than eighty percent water. We need great amounts of water in order to stabilize our system and cleanse it of toxic matter. Water is perhaps the most important thing that you can ingest. Water is the great cure-all. Water has long been known to prevent premature aging. It has properties in itself that can cure asthma, heartburn, lower back pain, angina, and migraine headaches. Water helps to keep your weight under control. Water also helps to reduce high blood pressure. There are hundreds of ailments that medicine has never been able to treat; however, water has been shown to cure or substantially alleviate many of these age-old sicknesses.

Most people do not take in the proper amount of water on a daily basis. Your body must be continuously hydrated in order for your internal organs to function properly. The general rule is to drink at least one-third of your body weight in ounces each day. For example, I weigh approximately 189 pounds. Thus, I need to drink at least sixty-three ounces of water every day to keep my body properly hydrated. That translates into about eight eight-ounce glasses of water every day. More than this minimum is, of course, beneficial to you.

Drinking soda or coffee does not count toward your targeted amount of water. The caffeine, sugars, and acids in these drinks can cause headaches, ulcers, and in some cases high blood pressure. In fact, because of the harmful substances in caffeinated beverages, you need to drink approximately three times as much water as you drank of soda and coffee, just to flush your system out. Of course, this water is in addition to your regular intake.

Make a commitment to your health to drink the daily requirement of water needed for your body. Plan to replace soda and coffee with water and natural juices. Natural juices are defined as juices that contain more than eighty percent juice and have no additives. Because our water systems have been contaminated with toxic chemicals, and many of our springs have become polluted, I suggest that you drink bottled distilled water.

Watch What You Eat

Some foods should be avoided because they have little or no nutritional value and thus cannot provide any beneficial elements in your physical functioning. In addition, they have been shown to cause major health problems in people.

The following list is not comprehensive. However, by simply eliminating these five foods from your diet, you can greatly improve your overall health:

1. Pork and pork products
2. Any food product containing hydrogenated oils, including peanut butters and margarine products
3. Sugar substitutes such as NutraSweet, Equal, and other artificial sweeteners
4. Any and all processed foods, junk food
5. All beverages containing caffeine

Of course, as you avoid these unhealthy foods, you will need to eat more fruits and vegetables and whole grains. It is preferable to eat foods that are organically grown, and that have been processed and cooked as little as possible.

Food Supplements

Your body craves and needs essential vitamins and minerals to function properly at the cellular level. It is impossible for any individual to regularly eat the quantity of food necessary to ingest the minimum levels of all the vitamins and minerals that the human body requires to function. In order to do this, a person would have to eat multiplied pounds of fruits and vegetables every day.

In light of this, everyone should take some form of dietary supplements. If this is new to you, you may want to begin with a good multivitamin that includes minerals. Find one that has been designed for your age and gender, because your needs can vary. If you are not able to swallow pills, there are many vitamin and mineral combinations that are available in liquid form.

This is only a start to fulfilling your supplemental needs. In time, you may advance to other healthy sources, such as liquid amino acids, aloe vera, colloidal silver, and even organic apple cider vinegar. By regularly taking essential vitamins and minerals, your body will begin the progress toward good health.

Fasting

Like water intake, fasting has great value for the body. I will list what I believe are some of the most important factors concerning fasting. We have already covered the spiritual benefits of fasting and prayer. Fasting also provides several natural, life-preserving benefits. Fasting purifies your entire system. When you fast for one or two days, the built-in healing power of your body starts to function. What happens in a fast is that all of the force that has been used to convert foods into energy and body tissue is now being used to rid the body of toxic poisons. These poisons are directly connected to many of the degenerative diseases from which we suffer. When we fast, we rid our bodies of the natural source of sickness, making us free from toxins and from the potential of contracting many deadly diseases.

Fasting gives your body a needed rest. Suppose you left your car running for five or ten years, during which time you stopped the engine just long enough to fill the gas tank and have the oil changed. Obviously, after a while your engine would blow up from overuse, abuse, and exhaustion. This is the same thing that happens when we eat continually, without giving our systems a break. Our bodies need rest from the massive labors of digesting and assimilating what we put into them. In addition, we have four principle organs that help eliminate waste from our systems:

the bowels, the kidneys, the lungs, and the skin. Fasting helps strengthen these vital organs, thus making it easier for us to function at full capacity.

Colon Cleansing

When you fast, you are allowing your colon the chance to rest and regain the energy it needs to process the food that you ordinarily consume. One way to neglect this essential organ is to put anything and everything into it. When people do not use discretion about what they eat, they will inevitably suffer from sickness and diseases. There are some foods that should never go inside the human body. These foods have no nutritional value at all. When they enter the digestive system, the colon tries to process the foreign matter without success. Food then remains in the colon to rot and harden on the colon walls.

In addition to fasting, you can take care of your colon with colon irrigation, also known as colon cleansing. A colon cleanse can be given one of two ways. You can take a colon cleanser internally through the mouth. This type of internal cleansing uses natural herbs in a tea or drink form to aid in washing the walls of the colon. Many people frown at the horrible taste and aftertaste of the procedure. This process, although effective, cannot be tolerated by everyone.

The second way is the colonic or colon irrigation, which is like a super-powered enema. It is a mobile power wash for your colon walls. A tube is inserted into the rectum, and gallons of distilled water flush the walls of the colon clean.

Once the walls of the colon have been cleaned, the colon can again retrieve the essential minerals and vitamins from the food we eat. A clogged colon blocks any possibility of natural health benefits and vitamin assimilation. You must keep your colon clean. This process is extremely effective in ridding the body of toxins that have built up in the system over many years. Colon irrigation should be administered by a person who is trained and certified to do this work. You may write to me for a list of certified technicians.

Sleep

We live in a society that absolutely thrives on making money. The lifestyle of the average New Yorker is a prime example of the hectic pace needed to fulfill this goal. Every minute in the day must be centered on some form of business. While this lifestyle may produce millions of dollars, it also greatly increases the mortality rate because it deprives the person of his crucial need for rest.

Sleep is as essential to a healthy body as eating food. Most people recognize the value of eating. Lack of food can cause death by starvation. In the same manner, lack of proper sleep can cause death by starving the body of its need for rest and restoration.

In 1996, I spent a few weeks in Egypt, studying ancient African civilizations and Nile valley religions. One day while touring and observing the wonderful city of Luxor, I noticed a mule that was carrying a heavy load, plus pulling a cart with the driver. First, this weight was far too much for the tiny mule to pull. Next, the mule had been pulling the weight all day long, twelve to fourteen hours a day. I saw the driver severely beating this beast with a goad stick. He beat the mule so severely that the flesh on its back began to bleed profusely. He was trying to get the mule to continue. The mule, under the pressures of heat, lack of water, and no rest at all, collapsed and died. The driver, not recognizing that the mule was dead, continued to beat the beast, even though it was not responding.

This man could have had the use of this mule for many more years if he had only understood and observed the law of rest. Obeying the law of rest has long-lasting, healthy consequences. Not understanding or repeatedly violating this law will often cause us to die long before our time.

Thus the heavens and the earth, and all the host of them, were finished. And on the seventh day God ended His work which He had done, and He rested on the seventh day from all His work which He had done. Then God blessed the seventh day and sanctified it, because in it He rested from all His work which God had created and made. (Genesis 2:1–3)

We should use God's example in Scripture concerning rest. God worked, and then He rested. Through His example we see that we earn rest. After we work with our minds and our physical bodies, our minds and bodies deserve rest. When we ignore this principle, our bodies will break down in tragic proportions.

Depending on age and work intensity, the average person needs six to eight hours of sleep each night. This amount may decrease with age, because many seniors lead a slightly slower lifestyle and are expending less energy as a result.

During the rest period, body cells are being recharged and repaired. Continued sleep deprivation will cause the cells to become damaged and irreparable in some cases. Although life may be full, take time to rest. If you do not take the time to rest, your body may take the time for you—eternally.

Exercise

Exercise is vitally important to your health and well-being. Exercise helps to normalize your blood pressure. It helps to unclog the arteries and veins, allowing blood to flow freely throughout the body. It burns away excess fat and improves your cholesterol profile. Exercise is the great stress reducer. Cancer and heart disease rates drop greatly for people who maintain a regular exercise schedule. It also increases your mental capacity for learning and understanding.

Everyone should exercise a minimum of three times a week for at least thirty minutes each session. There are many kinds of exercise from which to choose. Tae-bo, kickboxing, running, biking, tennis, basketball, and swimming are just a few popular forms of exercise. The exercise that you choose should be one that is safe for you and approved by your physician for your present physical condition.

Walking and swimming are perhaps the best overall exercises. When you walk or swim, nearly every muscle in your body is being worked. No other form of exercise provides as complete a workout as walking and swimming do.

Choose an exercise that will be to your personal liking, since you are the one who will do it.

It is not as important what exercise you choose as it is to make the choice to exercise.

Inactivity causes the body to become lethargic and unproductive. The lack of physical energy can lead to mental and emotional fatigue. Unnecessary health challenges can be brought on by a lack of exercise. The body needs daily stimulation for its muscles, tissues, and blood cells. Exercise makes this possible. Be sure to consult your physician first before beginning any exercise program.

Your Maintenance Program

God has designed our physical bodies to function in amazing ways. He has also provided healing for times when our bodies fail to function as He designed. Through His Word and the power of Christ, the Anointed One, we do have easy access to healing. However, with the gift comes responsibility; God expects us to maintain our physical health and to take care of our bodies so that we can better serve Him and build His kingdom.

**Maintain your maintenance program,
and it will maintain you.**

Afterthoughts:

Your God-given Destiny

Everything that we have discussed in these pages has to do with our hope in Christ Jesus. If you are in a situation where tragedy has hit you, it was not God who caused it. Still, there is hope even after tragedy. No matter what stage of life you are in, there is always hope. And that is what I am trying to foster—real hope, not false hope. The only false hope that exists is hope in the elements of this world and its systems. But hope in Christ is really our only hope. That's it. That is what I am communicating. There is no other real hope.

We live in a fallen world. We live in a world in which tragedy does strike. But I know that the only truth we can count on is that God can redeem us and heal our broken hearts and restore what the enemy has stolen.

Whether or not someone receives healing has nothing to do with the will of God to heal. God wants to heal us just as much as we want all of our children to be saved. We want all of our relatives to be saved, but unfortunately there will be some who still reject Christ, and so they won't be saved. They will go to hell for rejecting Christ, but that does not mean that it wasn't God's will for them to be saved. He says that it is His will that no one should perish.

> *The Lord is not slack concerning His*
> *promise, as some count slackness, but is*
> *longsuffering toward us, not willing that*
> *any should perish but that all should come*
> *to repentance.*   (2 Peter 3:9)

Some people are still going to perish. So how do you deal with that in light of this verse? Some are going to perish, but it is still God's will that they don't. Likewise, some people will never receive divine healing, but it is not because God doesn't want them to have it. Nothing can discount the nature and the power of God to heal.

There are some things that we can do within the realm of faith to activate the healing power of God, and there are some things that we have no power over. God is sovereign. He does what He wants to do because He is God. Even more so from our perspective, God sovereignly chooses to heal just because healing is a part of His nature.

About Prosperity

Because I serve in an inner city, multi-racial church, I hear far too many complaints from people of one race blaming people of a different race for being the reason why they can't profit in life. That type of empty talk lacks any validity. I want to scream against that falsehood because it perpetuates strife and because it ultimately is self-victimization.

The real reason why individuals don't prosper is because of ignorance concerning the laws of prosperity. Yes, there are some situations in which a person did not come from the best circumstances. Well, fine. Let's work with that. Let's work with the fact that you weren't born with a silver spoon in your mouth. You didn't start off in this region or that environment. Let's work with that. And then, let's grow.

You can grow from anywhere that you are. That statement takes away all excuses because it is God who prospers. It is God who heals. And He is no less than He has ever been. He is always going to be the same. So if we connect properly to Him, then we can get the supply that we need, whether it is healing or prosperity or relationships.

Everyone who has been made righteous by the blood of Jesus and who lives a righteous lifestyle according to Scripture should have good health and wealth as top priorities in his or her life. Of course, wealth comes from God so that you can establish His covenant on this earth.

We can't do anything—anything in the natural realm—that is going to be significantly blessed if we are continually sick, and we don't have money. So that is really what I believe about the hope found in 3 John 2. Health and prosperity have been downplayed for many, many years, and that is why the church has been sick and broke and not effective in reaching the world. We can't reach the people of the world if we are physically ill and we don't have money to finance the efforts.

I am definitely not putting health and wealth on a priority level above the righteousness of God. This is truly about Christ first, last, and always. Once I get into Christ, then and only then I will get these benefits. The fact is, however, that we need to start prioritizing health and wealth as necessities for getting the things of God done in our lives.

You were created to rule. God desires you to rule with strength and endurance. This will only be accomplished through physical bodies that are healthy and whole.

God intends that each of us will fulfill the destiny He has planned for us. My purpose in life is to provide the world with every workable spiritual and natural solution to the problem of sickness and disease. Thus, my destiny is to help you be able to fulfill your destiny.

It is my conviction that I am assigned to you. I am assigned to help you live to accomplish your goals, dreams, and purposes. I pray that I have served you sufficiently in bringing the message of healing to you.

More than that, I believe that you now have the weapons and tools you need to take this message of healing straight through the dawn of the twenty-first century to the coming of our Lord.

Times have changed, and people continually change. Healing will be as strong, even stronger, as we approach the return of our Lord. Our generation will witness the greatest healings that we have ever seen. One thing that will always remain the same is the Word of God.

Jesus Christ is the same yesterday,
today, and forever.
—Hebrews 13:8

About the Author

Pastor Aaron D. Lewis, a native of Connecticut, is celebrating more than ten years of pulpit ministry and evangelism. His spiritual conversion and training were forged in the fervency of Pentecostalism. Through the years, Pastor Aaron has served in numerous capacities in the body of Christ: as District Youth and Christian Education Director for the Church of God (Cleveland, TN), as a healing evangelist, as an entrepreneur, and as an accomplished musician.

As a healing evangelist, Pastor Aaron has traveled through the United States and internationally, conducting Schools of Healing and Miracle Awakening Healing Crusades. His anointed messages focus on the kingdom of God, healing, and fulfilling your God-given destiny. Through his ministry, God has performed many creative miracles and healed various diseases. As a result of God's anointing, hundreds of people have received salvation. Pastor Aaron has shared the stage with some of the finest ministers in this country and abroad, including Dr. Myles Munroe, Tim Storey, and Dr. Oral Roberts.

It is Aaron Lewis' objective to educate people throughout the world about the need to be in good health and to avoid anything that would hinder its attainment. Through natural and supernatural resources, Lewis provides a balanced yet effective approach to healing for the whole body. He is very deliberate about his conviction that God wants all people to be healed so they can fulfill their God-given destinies on this earth.

Pastor Aaron Lewis is the organizing pastor of The Family of God in East Hartford, Connecticut, a multi-ethnic, Word-based, post-denominational church. In conjunction with the church, he publishes a bi-monthly newsletter, *One Blood*. His first book, *The Prince of Preachers: Listen to the Voice,* was published in 1995.

Pastor Aaron is happily married to Minister Tiwanna Monique Lewis, who also serves in ministry with him. They have five beautiful children: Eryn, Amber, Judah Myles, Israel Isaiah, and Madonna Lauryn.